The Inner World
of Farm Animals

The Inner World *of* Farm Animals

THEIR AMAZING SOCIAL, EMOTIONAL, *and* INTELLECTUAL CAPACITIES

AMY HATKOFF

Foreword by JANE GOODALL

Afterword by WAYNE PACELLE,
PRESIDENT OF THE HUMANE SOCIETY OF THE UNITED STATES

STEWART, TABORI & CHANG
New York

Published in 2009 by Stewart, Tabori & Chang
An imprint of ABRAMS

Library of Congress Cataloging-in-Publication Data:
Hatkoff, Amy.
The inner world of farm animals : their amazing social, emotional,
and intellectual capacities / Amy Hatkoff.
    p. cm.
ISBN 978-1-58479-748-7
1. Livestock—Behavior. 2. Domestic animals—Behavior. 3. Animal
intelligence. I. Title.
SF756.7.H38 2009
636—dc22

        2008039694

Editor: Kristen Latta
Designer: Anna Christian
Production Manager: Tina Cameron

The text of this book was composed in Atma Serif.

Printed and bound in China.
10 9 8 7 6 5 4 3

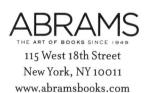

115 West 18th Street
New York, NY 10011
www.abramsbooks.com

This book is dedicated to farm animals everywhere
and to all those who are standing by, with, and for them.
It is my hope that as we come to see who they truly are,
we will be moved to act on their behalf.

And to my parents, Doris and Leon Hatkoff,
who taught me to listen with my heart.

"We have to understand that we are not the only beings on this planet with personalities and minds."

—Jane Goodall
Compassion in World Farming Conference

Contents

Foreword

THROUGHOUT MY CHILDHOOD I WAS FASCINATED WITH ANIMALS. At the age of ten I developed a very special relationship with an extraordinarily intelligent, mixed-breed dog, Rusty, who became my constant companion. He, along with the three successive cats, two guinea pigs, one golden hamster, one canary, and two tortoises, with whom we shared our house and our hearts, taught me that animals, at least those with reasonably complex brains, have vivid and distinct personalities, minds capable of some kind of rational thought and, above all, feelings.

Rusty was part of my life until his death. Soon after that I saved up and went to Africa, met the late Louis Leakey, and was offered the opportunity to study wild chimpanzees in Gombe National Park in Tanzania. As I began to learn about these apes, our closest living relatives, I was not at all surprised to find that they had extremely complex social lives, long-term bonds between family members and friends, and that in many ways, much of their behavior was uncannily like our own. And, as we know today, the biological similarities in composition of the blood and immune system, and structure of DNA, are extraordinary. So too is the anatomy of the chimpanzee brain, more like the human brain than that of any other living being. It should not surprise us, therefore, that they are capable of intellectual abilities once thought unique to us.

However, when I went to Cambridge University in the early 1960s (to pursue a PhD in ethology even though I had never been to college), the majority of scientists maintained that the behavior of all animals—except the human animal—was little more than a series of genetically coded responses to sensory stimuli. To attribute human-like behavior to non-human animals was to be guilty of anthropomorphism. I should have identified chimpanzees by numbers rather than names, and I should not have used terms like personality, mind, or emotions, since these things were uniquely human. But my new understanding of the chimpanzees, as well as my years with Rusty, had taught me otherwise, and I refused to accept reductionist explanations of complex behavior. It seemed obvious to me that there was no sharp line between human and chimpanzee—the difference was of degree and not kind. And this, of course, gives us a new respect not only for chimpanzees but for all the other amazing animals with whom we share this planet. Including farm animals.

New information makes it clear that pigs are as intelligent as dogs (more so than some!). It wasn't until it was scientifically "proved" that crows could solve a complex intellectual problem that the "bird brain" was considered capable of intellectual performances. In *The Inner World of Farm Animals*, Amy Hatkoff opens our minds to the true nature of farm animals, points out that they, too, are intelligent, sentient beings. She provides a way for these animals to "speak" for themselves.

It is a fact that most people have no idea how animals are treated in factory farms. Billions are kept in the most horrifying conditions in intensive farms, often called factory farms. In stinking, unsanitary, and unbelievably cramped spaces, poultry, pigs, cows, and other animals bred for meat or for products such as eggs and milk, can know no peace until they are killed (often in hideous pain). They are often fed growth hormones so that they grow faster or produce more milk or eggs in the shortest period of time. This rapid and unnatural growth is stressful and harmful for the animals (and incidentally the hormones may also adversely affect the health of the humans who eat the meat and eggs and drink the milk). We have lost all respect for the animals we eat—they are simply bred for food and we forget that they too have minds and feelings. When I learned about intensive farming, I found I was thinking about meat differently. I looked at the piece of animal on my plate, and it symbolized *fear*, *pain*, and *death*. I stopped eating it.

And there is something else. In the terrible conditions in factory farms, animals can only be kept alive when given prophylactic doses of antibiotics. Gradually more and more bacteria are building up resistance to more and more antibiotics, for they have gotten into the human food chain, and they are out in the environment. Intensive farming is developing *super bugs* and already some people have died when they got simple infections that proved resistant to all known antibiotics.

But while it is true that the inhumane conditions in which these innocent and helpless animals are kept may be damaging to our own health, it is the misery that they surely experience that make the whole industry so utterly unacceptable. From my childhood experiences on the farm, I know that pigs, cows, goats, ducks, and chickens have unique personalities. My grandson has many roosters and hens, and he can tell me the personality and special behaviors of each one of them. He has observed all kinds of amazing behavior. One of his hens flew up into the air and landed on the back of a crow that was attacking one of her chicks. The crow retreated, dismayed. And he has a turkey named Paul. I'm not sure he's terribly intelligent, but what he lacks in brains he makes up for in personality. He had two rabbits who, for years, shared our house behaving just like any other household pet. They were litter trained like cats and loved to jump up and be cuddled on our knees. James Herriot, the British veterinarian, talks of a pig who adopted a stray kitten and fed him along with her piglets. And there was a story on TV of the hen who tried desperately to nurture an abandoned litter of puppies— and was very distressed when they would not follow her to eat the grain she led them to!

Animals will teach us a lot if we will but watch them, learn from them. The great humanitarian, Albert Schweitzer, was deeply concerned about animals, and wrote that "we need a circle of compassion that includes animals too." St. Francis of Assisi, in addition to preaching to the birds, often rescued small vulnerable animals, including a lamb that was to be slaughtered, which he hid in the folds of his habit.

Many beings on this planet need advocates, especially those who cannot speak for themselves. This is the most important message in this book—that farm animals feel pleasure and sadness, excitement and resentment, depression, fear, and pain. They are far more aware and intelligent than we ever imagined and, despite having been bred as domestic slaves, they are individual beings in their own right. As such, they deserve our respect. And our help. Who will plead for them if we are silent?

Jane Goodall PhD, DBE
Founder, The Jane Goodall Institute & UN Messenger of Peace

Looking Back, Looking Forward

"Until he extends the circle of his compassion to all living things, man will not himself find peace."

—Albert Schweitzer, from The Philosophy of Civilization

THROUGHOUT HISTORY, OUR UNDERSTANDING OF ANIMALS AND OUR relationship to them has been questioned, explored, and debated. Originally, their nature and fate were argued primarily by philosophers. Pythagoras, the Greek mathematician who lived in the sixth century B.C., is considered to be the first animal rights philosopher. He believed in justice and respect for animals. In the fourth century B.C., Aristotle argued that non-human beings were not capable of thinking and therefore existed simply for our use. His theories shaped human attitudes toward animals for centuries. During the Age of Enlightenment, attitudes toward animals became more flexible. Some philosophers argued that animals were capable of thought and had awareness.

Our perception of animals is also shaped by religious beliefs. The Judeo-Christian view holds that only humans were created in God's image and that therefore, the purpose of animals is to be of service to mankind. Eastern religions hold some animals in high regard. It is well known, for example, that in India, cows are viewed and treated as sacred.

In the late 1800s, Charles Darwin changed the course of our thinking about animals forever. In his seminal book, *The Descent of Man*, he concluded that "humans and the 'higher animals' have the same senses, intuitions, and sensations, similar passions, affections, and emotions . . . the same faculties of imitation, choice, imagination, the association of ideas and reason though in very different degrees." He thought that animals might have an awareness of their own lives, a critical marker of higher thinking.

Today, the capacities of animals are being studied in universities, institutes, and organizations throughout the world. Although the focus has been primarily on wild animals, farm animals are now receiving attention. The findings are significant and are explored throughout this book. They confirm and even exceed what many people have long felt, experienced, and observed.

It is becomingly increasingly clear that farm animals have complex thoughts, deep emotions, and social skills and rituals not unlike our own. Chickens, turkeys, geese, ducks, cows, pigs, sheep, and goats are slowly becoming recognized as sentient beings. Sentience means being aware of oneself, one's surroundings, one's bodily sensations, and of the emotions corresponding to that awareness. It means having an awareness of other animals as well as of humans. Research shows that farm animals have a wide range of feelings, including loyalty, sadness, joy, and fear. There is now a significant body of research confirming that their intelligence is much greater than had been previously understood. The findings show that in some areas, farm animals are as smart or smarter than our beloved dogs and cats. They learn from one another, have excellent memories, and can plan for the future. Cows, for example, like challenges and get great satisfaction from solving them. Chickens are excellent strategists, and pigs can even be taught to play video games on the computer!

All of the statements in this book about the abilities of farm animals are founded on scientific evidence. This is due partly to the fact that, without documentation, many of their capacities would seem unbelievable. The book also tells the story of their abilities through people's individual experiences with the animals. As Marc Bekoff, Professor Emeritus of Ecology and Evolutionary Biology at the University of Colorado, Boulder, has commented, "The plural of anecdote is data." In the same way that a picture can be worth a thousand words, a single experience can reveal a profound truth.

One story in particular stands out for the impact it had on my thinking about farm animals. *The Vancouver Sun* reported an incident about a duck who grabbed a police officer by the pant leg, quacking loudly, seemingly desperate for his attention. At first the officer brushed the duck off and went on his way. The duck, however, was persistent. She approached him again, tugging and quacking. Once she had his attention, she ran over to a sewer grate and lay down on top of it. The officer followed her, and in the water below, discovered eight little ducklings who had apparently fallen through the grates. He called for help, the ducklings were rescued, and mother and babies made their way to safer waters.

This story encapsulates what I experienced over and over as I learned about the extraordinary and often unexpected abilities of farm animals. I interviewed scientists, researchers, and individuals working with chickens, ducks, geese, turkeys, cows, pigs, sheep, and goats throughout the United States, England, France, Australia, Canada, and many other countries. In conversation after conversation, I was struck by the richness of the animals' lives. The complexity of their communication, the sophistication of their problem-solving abilities, and the range of their emotions became very vivid. As hearing and reading became believing for me, I was both excited and saddened. I realized that our lack of recognition of who they are is a loss not only for the animals, but for us as well, and particularly for our children. How is it that we do not know about their cognitive abilities or how much they care for one another, their children, and, if given the opportunity, for humans? We have overlooked farm animals as sentient beings from whom we have much to learn—and more important, to whom we have so much to give.

It is easy not to think about farm animals, about who they are, what they experience or even what they mean to us. For those of us who are city dwellers, our only contact with living pigs, sheep, chickens, turkeys, ducks, geese, cows, sheep, and goats may be limited, making it even more difficult to develop an understanding of them.

For me, it wasn't until I visited a farm animal sanctuary—a refuge for abused, abandoned, and neglected farm animals—that all that I had learned came together on multiple levels. On a cold, cloudy day in April, a friend of mine and I drove to the Woodstock Farm Animal Sanctuary in upstate New York. As I arrived at the farm, I was welcomed by a white goat named Snowball who came right up to me, nuzzled his head into my leg, and escorted me as I visited the other animals. I held a blind chicken named Coco, who buried her head into the crook of my arm and started to coo as I gently rocked her. I was greeted by groups of chickens who seemed curious, communicative, and distinctly unique. I was surrounded by five exquisite turkeys who sat with me on the grass looking into my eyes as I stroked their feathers. I was amazed at how personable and engaging they were. Unfortunately, they had been bred to be overweight and were struggling to support their size. I hesitated to leave them, which turned out to be unnecessary as they never left my side. They accompanied me as I rubbed the bellies of pigs weighing 800 pounds. They escorted me to meet four large steer, who, despite their size and strength, gently lowered their heads so I could scratch behind their ears. The turkeys stood by me as I sat with a goat named Olivia who had been diagnosed with cancer, but was filled with sweetness and light.

What struck me was that I found myself relating to and interacting with these animals in the same way I do with the dogs and cats in my life. They were no different. They were just as present, aware, engaging, warm, friendly, nervous, funny, or shy. Yet in so many ways, these animals are the forgotten ones, the ones we rarely see, hear, touch, or get to know. In these two short hours, however, they had become my teachers. With a majesty and grace that belied what they had been through, they seemed to represent the possibility of hope, forgiveness, resilience, and an extraordinary ability to overcome. They had opened my heart and my mind to farm animals even further.

This book is dedicated to them and to the twenty-two billion animals who are currently being farmed throughout the world, often under conditions that are harsh and inhumane. It is written in the hope that as we discover who these animals are, we will be inspired to become part of the growing movement to treat them with much deserved compassion and respect.

The way we view animals determines how they are treated. Replacing common misconceptions with attitudes based on scientific data takes time and great effort. But the evidence demonstrating that farm animals are sentient beings is strong and undeniable. Many of the capacities that have long been thought unique to humans have been shown to be abilities that we share with non-human animals. Slowly, the walls separating "us" and "them" are coming down. We are beginning to recognize that these walls were, in fact, largely man-made. We are, indeed, closer than we think.

CHAPTER ONE

Chickens

Research confirms that chickens, who have traditionally been viewed as unintelligent, are capable of complex thought. Studies are now revealing that the avian brain is very similar to the human brain and processes information in much the same way. While other surprising capacities of chickens, such as their bravery and devotion to their offspring, have been addressed in literature as far back as the first century, for the most part the inner lives of chickens remain unsung.

I remember my past, and I think about my future.

"CHICKENS MAKE MEMORIES, as all animals do," comments Lesley Rogers, Emeritus Professor at the Centre for Neuroscience and Animal Behavior at the University of New England. "In fact, chicks can make memories even before they hatch." As embryos, they hear their mothers' vocalizations and are then able to identify and understand them when they are born.

As soon as they hatch, chicks are able to remember that something exists even if they are unable to see it. This is referred to as *object permanence* and is something that human infants are unable to do until they are five to eight months old. Italian researchers Giorgio Vallortigara of the University of Trento and Lucia Regolin of the University of Padua demonstrated this capacity by familiarizing chicks with red balls, which they then hid behind one of two screens. After a delay of sixty seconds, the chicks were able to remember behind which screen to look. "This ability is important," comments Rogers, "because one of the capacities we have associated with consciousness or higher cognition is the ability to think about something that is not in your immediate vicinity—such as things that happened yesterday, or what might happen tomorrow, or about what's happening around the corner."

Like other farm animals, chickens can tell people apart and remember their experiences of them. Researchers at the University of Guelph showed that chickens turned away from people who repeatedly withheld food from them. If they have been given a food reward for certain behaviors, they will give a cry of frustration if they don't receive the reward for the same behavior. This indicates that they expect things to occur based on past experience, a sign of higher thinking.

Chickens also have a sense of the future. Given a choice between receiving a small amount of food immediately or a larger amount in the future, they will choose the latter, demonstrating self-control and the capacity to delay gratification.

> **"... the chick possesses one of the characteristics essential for being an individual. It can acquire information and encode memories. ... It is the collection of memories that becomes part of the self."**
>
> —Lesley Rogers, from **Minds of Their Own: Thinking and Awareness in Animals**

We like to hang out together.

CHICKENS ARE VERY SOCIAL and form strong friendships. They prefer the company of familiar chickens and avoid chickens they don't know. As soon as they hatch, chicks are able to recognize their siblings, and they choose to stay with them. Even at three days old they recognize other chicks with whom they are raised and prefer their company to that of unfamiliar chickens. "When we look at chickens, they all look very similar. Obviously by the chicks, individuals are easily discriminated," comments Professor Rogers. "Just like humans, the more experience you have with looking at different faces, the better you become at discriminating one face from another."

According to "Sentient Beings," a report by Farm Sanctuary, "Being in the company of their peers may be even more important to chickens than food. When researchers placed chicks at the start of a long runway they approached a video of other chicks much faster than they approached a video of a box of food." Studies have shown that when a pair of chicks is separated, their stress hormones become elevated. If given the opportunity, chicks who have been separated from their mothers will stay with their siblings through the night.

Notorious Boy and Mary: A Love Story

Mary was an older hen who was found in a city dump and brought to live at Animal Place, a farm sanctuary in Vacaville, California. There she met and bonded immediately with Notorious Boy, a rooster who had been found abandoned on a nearby property. "Notorious Boy's personality can best be described as 'wonderfulness,'" comments Kim Sterla, co-founder and director of the sanctuary. "Most of the roosters will try to get as many hens as they can, but Notorious Boy was only interested in his Mary. He was very tender and attentive to her. He would always call her over for the food treats before eating any himself. They spent every day and night together, off on their own." They particularly liked to roost on a wooden picnic table in Sterla's backyard. One night during a heavy storm, Sterla looked out her window to make sure that they were out of the rain. There she saw them still perched on the bench, but Notorious Boy had completely covered Mary with his wing. "This is how mother hens sleep with their chicks," continues Sterla. "It was the most precious thing I had ever seen. The bond between them was immense. They had what appeared to be a loving, respectful relationship, with absolutely no interest in others. They have both passed away, but I will never forget them."

Co-op or Condo?

WHEN A HEN is about to lay an egg, she signals her mate with a nesting call. According to Karen Davis, founder and president of United Poultry Concerns, the rooster and hen will then search together for a place where they can build their nest. If the rooster likes a spot, he snuggles into it, rocks from one side to the other, and emits a "grumbling" sound. The hen also has to approve or they continue their search.

Davis points out that the rooster is actually a family man. She describes him as "a lover, a father, a brother, a food-finder, a guardian, and a sentinel." Ulisse Aldrovandi, a sixteenth-century natural historian, commented that the rooster "is for us the example of the best and truest father of a family."

"As I watched and got to know the chickens, I was so surprised to see how much they interacted with each other. I realized that they had likes and dislikes and friends and boyfriends and girlfriends, just like we do."

—Terry Cummings, founder and co-director, Poplar Spring Animal Sanctuary

Charlie Parker: Another Bird

Charlie Parker was rescued by the Eastern Shore Sanctuary when he was a baby chick. When he first arrived, he didn't know how to interact with other chickens and became very attached to Pattrice Jones, the sanctuary's founder, who he treated like his mother. He hid between her legs, jumped up and sat on her lap, and chased after her if she left the chicken yard. In hopes that he would begin to relate to other chickens if with a smaller group, Jones placed young Charlie in the infirmary area, where he met Che Guevera, an older rooster who had been badly injured.

Che literally took Charlie under his wing, and when he did so, Charlie, who was excitable and anxious, was visibly calmed and comforted.

Eventually, Che died, and as Charlie aged, he developed medical problems himself. He was taken to the infirmary, and history repeated itself. Charlie became the one who comforted the new arrivals, taking them one by one under the shelter of his wings. This is something roosters rarely do. Charlie had clearly learned well and seemed able to pass along the gift he had received.

We learn by watching.

MUCH OF A BABY CHICK'S BEHAVIOR is learned rather than instinctual, as previously thought. Research has shown that chickens, as well as other farm animals, pass cultural knowledge along to their offspring. This had long been considered unique to human intelligence.

As soon as her chicks hatch, a mother hen teaches them about which foods to eat and which to avoid. She does this by example and by redirection. If she sees her chicks eating food that is not healthy, she will peck and scratch to guide them toward a healthier food. If she discovers that a food is unpalatable, she will avoid it and teach her chicks to do the same. She also teaches them about safety and avoiding enemies.

Not only do chicks learn by watching their mothers, they learn from one another as well. Research has shown that at just one day old, chicks will avoid eating bitter-tasting food simply by seeing another chick's negative reaction to it.

Chickens also learn from watching videos! Researchers at the University of Bristol have shown chickens a video of a hen with two bowls of food, one red and one yellow. In the video, the hen eats only from the red bowl. When these two colored bowls of food are presented to different groups of chickens who were shown the video, they will repeatedly eat only from the red bowl.

"Until very recently, scientists were still advancing the idea that most creatures behave by sheer instinct, and that what appeared to be learned behavior was merely genetically wired activity . . . in fact, we are finding out that learning is passed on from parent to offspring far more often than not and that most animals engage in learned experience brought on by continued experimentation and trial-and-error problem solving."

—Jeremy Rifkin, president, Foundation on Economic Trends

Violet and Chickweed: A Painful Parting

Rescued at a very young age by the Eastern Shore Sanctuary in Maryland, this brother and sister team was very attached. They stayed together day and night, watching over each other protectively. Sadly, Violet died suddenly from an undetected infection. "Chickweed was devastated," comments Pattrice Jones. "He watched us bury Violet and, for the next several weeks, would return to stand silently at the place from which he had last seen her. Like many people do when they are mourning, he became angry and would rage around the yard every day. At night, he would stand in the coop alone, drooping with sadness. While he became less angry over time, he was never the same as he had been before Violet died."

I'm no birdbrain!

"IT IS NOW CLEAR that birds have cognitive capacities equivalent to those of mammals, even primates," comments Professor Rogers in her book, *The Development of Brain and Behaviour in the Chicken*. Rogers discovered that chickens use the right and the left sides of their brains for different functions. This is referred to as *lateralization* and had been thought to be unique to humans and essential for tool use, language, and consciousness.

Chickens have complex cognition and can grasp abstract concepts. Giorgio Vallortigara of the University of Trento and Lucia Regolin of the University of Padua have shown that chicks are capable of recognizing a whole object even when it is partly hidden. This is a capacity it was thought only humans possessed. Human babies can only begin to do this at four months of age, while chicks can do it when they are just two or three days old. "When human babies do this, it is seen as a milestone of cognitive development," comments Rogers. "But chicks can do it from the word go."

Chickens can also follow the direction of eye gazes, another example of their capacity for higher thinking. As Professor Rogers points out, in order to do this, one has to first have an awareness that others exist and then grasp that they are looking at something.

Chickens have even demonstrated the ability to count! Vallortigara and Regolin with Rosa Rugani of the University of Padua, trained chicks to peck for food at the fourth container in a series of ten containers. They then changed the spacing between the containers so that they were all in different positions. The chicks, however, were still able to select the fourth container, meaning they were able to identify the container through counting rather than relying on its location. The researchers proved the chickens' ability to count in other experiments as well.

Vallortigara and his colleagues also found that chickens can perform basic geometry. They placed chicks in a rectangular room with an object in one corner. They then removed the object and the chicks from the room and brought the chicks back with the task of identifying the corner in which the object was previously located. This is an extraordinarily difficult task with no straightforward solution. Chicks, however, can solve this problem with ease. The researchers believe that the chickens use the different lengths of the walls and the angular positions to reorient themselves. They can learn, for instance, that the correct corners are the ones with a short wall on the left and a long wall on the right.

Vallortigara and Luca Tommasi of the University of Chieti discovered another example of chickens' ability to use geometric information. After learning to find food placed in the center of a square-shaped area, chickens were able to find the centers of other geometrically shaped areas that had no food.

Chickens also like stimulation and new information. According to "Sentient Beings," a report by Farm Sanctuary, chickens were shown two screensavers with different images, flying toasters and fish, for different lengths of time. When the researchers showed the chicks both screens again, the chicks chose to watch the screen they had seen for a shorter period of time. Human infants have also been shown to seek out novel experiences. They will choose to view new images rather than ones with which they are already familiar.

"Chickens follow their chicks with such great love that if they see any harmful animal . . . stalking their little ones, the hens gather them under the shadow of their wings. They would rather die for their chicks than seek safety in flight."

—Ulisse Aldrovandi, natural historian, sixteenth century

No Greater Love

In his book, *Call Me Chicken*, Reverend L. Joseph Tauer tells the story of his hen, Liza, the proud mother of six newly hatched baby chicks. One day, Tauer was looking out the window and saw Liza and his other hens running for cover from a hawk who was hovering above. He then saw Liza running back into the open field. Her baby chicks did not know the alarm call and were still feeding on the grass. Tauer watched as Liza crouched down and covered her chicks with her wings to protect them from the hawk's attack. He ran outside and was greatly relieved to see all of the chicks poke their heads out from under their mother.

Then to his utter relief, he saw Liza spread her wings to reveal that she too survived.

"I had just witnessed a chicken perform a deed that would make headlines if the same act had been performed by a human," recounts Tauer. "The phrase entered my mind, 'No greater love.' Would I have measured up? Here was a creature that many educated and philosophic people have declared not only to have no soul, but to be without the capability of thinking or reasoning. Yet, Chicken, judged and found lacking by humans, had just performed the supreme heroic and selfless act."

We bond before birth.

THE BOND BETWEEN A MOTHER HEN and her chicks is forming while the chicks are still embryos, a time during which they are already engaged in back-and-forth responsive communication. "About twenty-four hours before a chick is ready to hatch, it begins to peep in its shell to notify its mother and siblings that it is ready to emerge," comments Karen Davis. The mother responds to their peeps by covering her unborn chicks with her body or by making soothing sounds. This communication continues until hatching. Siblings also communicate with one another before they hatch. While embryos, chicks emit different sounds that can actually speed up or slow down each other's development. This can also result in their hatching at the same time.

Baby chicks who are removed from their mothers will call and search for them. Upon hearing their distress, the mother, if able, will return their call. "Should a peep be missing or sound frightened," says Davis, "she runs to find the chicks."

We know what's important to us.

MARION STAMP DAWKINS, author of *Through Our Eyes Only?: The Search for Animal Consciousness*, has devoted her career to the study of the intelligence of animals, particularly chickens. She is the pioneer of what is known as *preference work*, in which researchers ask the animals themselves what they want and how much they want it. This information can then be used to understand and better meet the animals' needs. Dawkins discovered, for example, that chickens would work to push themselves through a small space in order to be with their litter or reach their nest, but they wouldn't push themselves through the space to reach their mates. Preference work has also shown how important dust-bathing is to chickens. They will peck keys one hundred times to get access to a space where they can clean themselves by rolling about and spreading their wings in the dust, as compared to pecking only ten times to gain access to a space that contains hard objects such as thumbtacks.

Chickens also know what is good for them. Chickens in pain, for example, will choose and continue to eat foods laced with painkillers. When they recover, however, they will then select food without the drugs.

Brandy: A True Gentleman

Brandy was rescued from a hatchery in Pennsylvania when he was just a baby chick. He had been put into a plastic bag and left near a dumpster along with several other male chicks. After seven years at one sanctuary, he was brought to the Woodstock Farm Animal Sanctuary in upstate New York. He was very people-friendly from the moment he arrived. "Brandy was truly an ambassador for all of 'roosterdom,'" comments Jenny Brown, co-founder of the sanctuary. "He was a guy who would walk right up to you and without flinching or flopping let you pick him up and hold him. He would run, not walk, whenever I called his name. One of

the most remarkable things about Brandy is that he was an incredible gentleman. Good roosters, like good husbands," continues Brown, "bring any food they find to the ladies. If Brandy found something—a grub, a worm, or food we'd given him—instead of eating it for himself, he'd go out of his way to call the ladies over. He'd make a bunch of noise and this crazy sound. They would come running, and he would take the morsel up and drop it several times and do his little scratching dance until one of the ladies ate it."

A boy named Will who had cerebral palsy visited the sanctuary frequently. Will loved Brandy, and while roosters do not usually sit in anyone's lap, Brandy would sit in Will's and let him pet him.

Brandy would frequently visit Jenny in her house for an afternoon treat. He'd let her bring him onto the couch where she would often stroke his chin as he lay next to her. Jenny describes Brandy as a "complex fella." He died in her arms.

> **"Animals are versatile in response to new challenges; they communicate requests, answer questions, and express emotions."**
>
> —Jonathan Balcolmbe, from **Pleasureable Kingdom**

We have a lot to say.

CHICKENS HAVE HIGHLY DEVELOPED communication skills. According to Dr. Gisela Kaplan, a professor at the University of New England, "the voices of birds involve learned, complex vocalizations." Researchers have identified more than thirty-one different call types with very specific meanings. Chickens use separate alarm calls, for example, depending on whether a predator is traveling by land or in the sky. Karen Davis of United Poultry Concerns describes numerous calls, including distress calls, nesting and mating calls, laying calls, threat calls, "all clear" calls, contented calls, and contact calls. Davis comments that "each rooster can recognize the crow of at least thirty other roosters, probably more." Australian scientists recently discovered that some hens emit high-pitched sounds to signal they have found food. The more they prefer a particular food, the faster they "speak."

Jonathan Balcolmbe, senior research scientist at Physicians Committee for Responsible Medicine, explains that "roosters sometimes make a 'come hither' call. Recognizing the call, a hen comes running and the rooster gallantly points out a grasshopper or some other morsel in the grass. By treating the ladies, a rooster may improve his chances of a future mating opportunity. But roosters are not always so noble; sometimes they'll fake it, delivering a 'come hither' call when there's no treat there. The hen, unaware of the deception, comes running only to find that there's nothing there. But it doesn't pay a rooster to deceive too often for he may soon be identified by equally alert hens as unreliable."

Chris Evans of Australia's Macquarie University, and Peter Marler, formerly of University of California, Davis, found that when different predator alarm calls are played back on a tape to hens or roosters, they make the appropriate response calls. However, they will only emit a warning call if there is another chicken present to hear it. This is referred to as *audience effects* and is another indication of intentionality in their communication.

Recognition of this level of complexity in a chicken's communication was considered groundbreaking. "Until very recently, we believed only primates were capable of such sophisticated communication," comments Professor Kaplan. "It proves that birds have a semantic way of communicating, and these are the rudiments of language."

CHAPTER TWO

Geese, Ducks, and Turkeys

While ducks are thought to be cute and geese can appear elegant, turkeys are not generally considered appealing. When presented with the opportunity to meet them, however, people are often surprised to discover just how grand they are. Iridescently colored and exquisitely plumed, they frequently have friendly, engaging personalities. They can also be affectionate, and have been known to "hug" humans. Geese display concern for one another and are faithful to their "spouses." Ducks are social and some even have a sense of humor.

We are very loyal.

WHEN GEESE MATE, they tend to remain monogamous, looking for a new partner only if their mate dies. Some geese will remain alone by choice for the rest of their lives, which can be as long as twenty-five years. They are also very protective of their family members. If a goose's mate or gosling becomes sick or injured, she will often refuse to leave their side. Occasionally, this protective instinct will take priority over her own survival, and she will stay with her loved one in need, even when the rest of the flock migrates south for the winter. If a goose's eggs are destroyed, she will mourn, often isolating herself from others.

Konrad Lorenz—considered one of the founders of ethology, the study of animal behavior—discovered that geese exhibit the same physical signs of grief as humans. Their eyes sink, their bodies droop, and their heads hang.

We back each other up.

IN ADDITION TO BEING LOYAL to their mates, geese are also known to be cooperative with and supportive of one another. Flying in a "V" formation helps each bird fly more quickly than if they flew alone. According to the Humane Society of the United States, the geese take turns relieving the head goose when it tires. While in this formation the leading birds also receive honks of encouragement to keep up their speed from those in the rear. If one of the geese is injured during flying, other members have been known to stay behind and care for the injured goose.

"Animals share with us the privilege of having a soul."
—Pythagoras

I believe in love at first sight.

IMPRINTING IS A PROCESS by which a newborn becomes attached to a parental figure. Its effects are irreversible and last a lifetime. In the case of turkeys, it occurs 12 to 24 hours after hatching. The attachment, however, is not always to a parent.

Joe Hutto, a naturalist who has lived with many species of animals, was present at the hatching of fourteen wild turkeys, who imprinted on him. He then spent two years with them in Northern Florida as their "mother." Hutto kept a diary of his experience and observations, which he recounts in his book, *Illumination in the Flatwoods: A Season with the Wild Turkey*.

Hutto recalls how the young turkeys, known as poults, became very attached to him and would panic if they could not see him: "I had to be in their physical presence as long as they were awake. It was devastating for them for me to be away from them. If I left them, it would wreck them. I had made my turkey bed, and I had to sleep in it."

William M. Healy, PhD, former Research Wildlife Biologist with the United States Forest Service, is referred to as the pied piper of wild turkeys. In order to get close enough to study them, Healy, like Hutto, became "mother" to several broods. After the hatching of one brood, he recounts taking the poults directly out of an incubator and driving with them in his pockets to his lab, keeping them warm and comforted. Healy points out that imprinting doesn't change the behavior: rather, it only changes the object toward which it is directed. At the lab, the poults began to peep, peep, peep at Healy. This sound is known as the "lost call" and is used to signal the mother. Hutto translates it to mean, "You're my mom, I need you. Come closer."

"... the mother is the center of the young bird's universe. ... Wild turkey poults are as dependent on a mother or parent substitute as their domesticated counterparts to get a proper start in life."

—Karen Davis, founder and president, United Poultry Concerns

Let's talk turkey!

TURKEYS, LIKE CHICKENS AND OTHER BIRDS, have well-developed vocabularies. "They recognize one another by their voices as well as their head characteristics," comments William Healy. "To turkeys, the voices of other turkeys are unique and recognizable."

More than twenty distinct vocalizations have been identified among wild turkeys. Each one is very specific, with subcategories and slight variations in meaning. Hutto always knew his brood had found a rattlesnake because they had a very specific call that applied only to that type of snake. Turkeys can tell the difference between a soaring vulture, eagle, or hawk, and have distinct vocal responses to each.

Turkeys can also communicate their emotions to one another. A turkey's snood, which hangs down from its forehead, is featherless and changes colors according to its emotional state. The colors range from white to red to blue. Chickens also show emotions in the skin on their neck or face.

"Turkeys display immense affection toward humans. They love to be caressed, and people often remark that they respond just like their own dogs and cats. Turkeys even make a purring sound when they are content.

Some turkeys are more affectionate than others, climbing into your lap and making themselves as comfortable as can be. At Farm Sanctuary in California, a particularly friendly turkey named Lydia became known for her propensity to hug. As soon as you crouched down, she would run over to you, press her body against yours, and crane her head over your shoulders, clucking all the while. It's amazing how so generous a hug can be given by something with no arms."

—Colleen Patrick-Goudreau, founder of Compassionate Cooks

Alice: A Turkey with Many Loves

Alice lives at the Poplar Spring Animal Sanctuary in Maryland. She is described as "one of a kind" with a fascination with wheels. "When parents were pushing their children in the strollers for the tours, Alice would get really excited and run next to them," comments Terry Cummings, founder of the sanctuary. "The parents who didn't know her would be scared, thinking that she was after the babies, but she just wanted to be next to the wheels on the strollers. She also liked wheelchairs because they had really big wheels; she would sit down next to a handicapped person, and they were all excited because they got to pet her, but she was just excited because she got to be next to the wheels." Alice also loved people, especially children. "She'd join all of the tours and walk around the whole farm with everybody," continues Cummings. "She would get all excited when the tour buses came and would run to the top of the hill to wait for the kids to come out. One time the kids were acting up and the teacher ordered them to get in a single-file line and back onto the bus. To everybody's surprise, Alice got in line and marched right onto the bus with all of the kids." Alice also had a love of

dancing. "When we had our open houses, she would get up and strut and turn around and dance with all of the bands playing."

We know the lay of the land.

IN *ILLUMINATIONS IN THE FLATWOODS*, Joe Hutto describes the cognitive abilities of wild turkeys in numerous arenas. He comments that "the most important activity of a young wild turkey is the acquisition and assimilation of information. . . . They are curious to a fault, they want a working understanding of every aspect of their surroundings, and their memory is impeccable. They gather specific information about a particular environment, conspicuously apply that information to a framework of general knowledge, and make appropriate choices in modifying their behavior."

William Healy concurs that turkeys are excellent at geography. They quickly learn to navigate the places they frequent daily. Given the opportunity, they can learn the details of a terrain of more than one thousand acres in the course of a year and keep that information in mind. They are very perceptive and acutely aware if something in their environment changes.

"If I had to sum up my experience with the wild turkey, the most profound thing that I discovered is that they are so much more complex in their intelligence, their behavior, and their problem-solving ability than I ever imagined. They are sentient beings. By every measure and every definition of intelligence, in their environment and in their world, they were without question so much more intelligent than I was. The time I spent with them was this wonderful kind of humiliation. We are not superior beings, we are just different beings. We are not more interesting creatures."

—Joe Hutto

Peepers: The People's Duck

Peepers, a duck found living in a tiny cardboard box, was rescued by the Catskill Animal Sanctuary in Saugerties, New York. Overwhelmed and terrified of people when he first arrived, Peepers was placed in a separate area where the staff spent hours patiently reassuring him and letting him come to them when he felt ready. Eventually, he'd come out from his enclosure a little bit at a time but, like a child, he'd run right back. After a few months of continuous TLC, Peepers made it all the way down the long barn aisle. There he saw the pond and the fields, but again, he ran right back to his box. "Over time, he completely came out of his shell and became so under foot it was amazing," comments Kathy Stevens, the sanctuary's founder. "Wherever we were, he wanted to be. He had no interest in other ducks. He only wanted to be with humans." Peepers was finally adopted by a loving family. His typical night is relaxing with them on the sofa and sitting in someone's lap as they watch the evening news.

Different quacks for different folks!

SCIENTISTS IN GREAT BRITAIN have recently discovered that, like humans, ducks have regional accents. For example, city ducks have a "shouting" quack that is thought to compensate for the noise of the city. Country ducks' quacks are softer. Victoria de Rijke, lecturer in English at Middlesex University in England, who led the research, comments that she ". . . chose ducks because they are so like humans—they are very sociable, they have a good sense of humor, and they are birds of habit."

CHAPTER THREE

Cows

Cows have had a long, enduring relationship with humans. Domesticated more than 8,000 years ago, under the right circumstances they live harmoniously and cooperatively with one another. If given the opportunity, they form close and long-lasting relationships. These powerful but gentle creatures possess surprising emotional qualities. They are perceptive, sensitive, and highly attuned to one another. They are even thought to grieve at the loss of their bovine family or friends. Farmers have long observed the strength of their maternal bonds as well as their distress when these bonds are broken.

I love an intellectual challenge.

RESEARCH SHOWS that cows enjoy solving problems. In an experiment led by Donald M. Broom, professor of animal welfare at Cambridge University, young dairy cows appeared to be excited when they successfully learned how to unlatch a gate to obtain food. Their heart rates accelerated and their behavior became more animated. Some of the cows even jumped! Professor Broom and his colleagues described it as a "eureka" moment for the cows. The group that received the food without unlatching the gate did not show these changes in their behavior or heart rates.

These findings indicate that it is possible that cows have an emotional reaction to their own learning and achievement. This is particularly significant because it indicates that they have self-awareness, one of the key components of consciousness.

"There is no fundamental difference between man and the higher animals . . . in their mental facilities."
—Charles Darwin, from **The Descent of Man**

We value our friendships.

COWS, LIKE ALL FARM ANIMALS, have a strong need for social interaction. They form close relationships with several cows within their herd. They have distinct preferences, usually for cows of their own age or with whom they have been raised. They spend most of their time together, standing by one another, sharing food, coordinating activities, and grooming one another.

Studies have shown that being together provides cows with emotional and social support, helping them feel secure and comforted, particularly in times of stress. When cows are with their "friends," they are more resilient and less frightened by new situations. They also learn more quickly when they are with other cows than when they are alone.

Being separated is stressful and has a negative impact on their health, well-being, and productivity. It results in an increase in their heart rates and their levels of stress hormones. When separated, cows will call out and walk back and forth rapidly in an effort to reconnect with one another. This is similar to human babies crying when separated from their parents, as described by John Bowlby, the father of attachment theory.

We are decision makers.

SEVERAL RESEARCHERS HAVE EXPLORED how cows and other farm animals make numerous decisions and need to do so for survival and well-being. According to Professor Broom, "Social animals such as cattle, sheep, and pigs need substantial intellectual ability in order to cope with their complex social life." Broom explains that the simple act of eating requires a series of decisions, including where to find food and which food to eat or avoid. Cows also need to remember where the good grazing spots are located and to know when to return to those spots after the grass has grown back.

Cows have been shown to understand cause and effect and can learn to press a lever for food when they are hungry and push a button for water when they are thirsty.

They are also being taught to "read" to help them make informed decisions. Jenny Jago, a scientist at Dexcel in New Zealand, and her colleagues are teaching cows to go through gates using signs to identify the correct one. The cows are beginning to understand what the signs mean. The researchers are trying to determine the criteria upon which the cows are basing their decisions and exploring if the cows are using the cues of shape or color.

> **"We have found over the years that if they are allowed the right conditions to live in, cattle make very good decisions."**
>
> —Rosamund Young, from **The Secret Life of Cows**

Durham: Singing for His Supper

Durham, an underweight calf living at Kites Nest Farm in England, was given an extra feeding each day in an effort to help him put on weight. Apparently, he learned to distinguish between staff members and remember who fed him each day. According to Rosamund Young, who runs the farm with her family, Durham "never asked the same person twice for food on the same day, but if a different person approached him he would try pretending for all he was worth that he had not been fed that day."

We learn from each other.

COWS LEARN FROM ONE ANOTHER, a trait common to most farm animals, and one of the most complex forms of learning. Research by Derek Bailey, associate professor of animal and range sciences at New Mexico State University, has demonstrated that 81 percent of cows who discover where food is located by following a leader in a maze can later find that site on their own.

Cows are also influenced by one another and can be encouraged to avoid or to try new things by another's behavior. Just seeing a cow receive a shock from an electric fence, for example, is enough to deter other cows from approaching it themselves. Like chickens, cows have been shown to try new foods or avoid harmful ones by observing one another.

Cows Using Tools?

Joe Stookey of the University of Saskatchewan and his research group have been studying ways to reduce the stress caused by abrupt weaning of calves. They have tried "fence-line weaning," a method in which the cows and calves are able to maintain some contact by being kept on opposite sides of a common fence. Even with the close contact, the cows are still visibly upset by the separation. Stookey and his group count the vocalizations of the cows as an indicator of their stress levels.

Stookey explains, "Most of the time the cows and calves will stand facing each other and call, but sometimes we noticed the cows would enter the tin shed where it was impossible for them to see their calf and begin a long and loud series of calls. We wondered why they would do this because it would have been easier to see their calf and 'talk' to it if they would go nearer to the fence. Several times we observed cows at the corner location of the shed swing their heads into the shed where they would begin a long series of calls, and when they finished calling they would swing their head out of the tin shed and look toward the calves. The calls always seemed louder when made inside the shed, where they echoed and reverberated against the tin sides and roof, and we wondered if the cows were intentionally using the tin shed to make their calls louder! If that is what they were in fact trying to do, then it loosely fits the definition of tool use in animals as defined by biologists. Tool use in animals is always of interest because it represents higher cognitive thinking on the part of the animal. In scientific terms this is a very anecdotal story with a very liberal interpretation on our part about the behavior we observed, but it certainly elevates my curiosity and excitement to think that perhaps cows could enter the category of another reasoning animal that uses tools."

Milking with Mozart

When Daniel McElmurray was ten years old, he wanted to help his father improve the lagging milk production of the three hundred cows on their dairy farm in Georgia. Knowing he and his father enjoyed listening to music as they milked the cows, Daniel thought the cows might enjoy it, too. But he wanted to find out what kind of music they

would like. He played rock, country, and classical music during the daily milking. After listening to the classical music, the cows produced one thousand pounds more milk. "I think the slower music helps them relax," commented Daniel, whose research won him first prize at a regional science fair.

I can keep things in mind.

COWS HAVE EXCELLENT MEMORIES. They can keep at least fifty bovine faces and ten human faces in mind for several years. They can also tell people apart, relying mostly on visual cues such as clothing, colors, faces, and height. They can distinguish people based on their posture and the way they move. Even young calves are able to recognize differences in people.

Cows can remember the location of things in their environment such as migration paths, shelter, water, fences, and grazing spots. "Cows can quickly learn these things and remember them for long periods," comments Derek Bailey, who, along with his colleagues, devised two differently shaped mazes to determine a cow's capacity to remember. They placed buckets of grain in different spots in each maze. The cows found and ate the food in the buckets, and they almost never returned to one they had already emptied. "Prior to these experiments, cows' movements were thought to be random," comments Bailey. "We didn't realize that they were forming a mental map and basing their current choices on their previous experiences. What this meant was that they had a working memory and were able to keep track of information."

Dylan and Friends: Hard to Say Good-bye

Bob Esposito, photographer and a good friend of the Woodstock Farm Animal Sanctuary, describes how cows are affected when one of their group members leaves at the end of the day: "During the daytime, Dylan stands, walks, nibbles hay, grooms, lies, and generally hangs out with the boys, Andy, Ralphie, and Elvis. But when the gate is opened and Dylan leaves to spend the evening with his goat friend, the group is genuinely affected by his departure. They usually stand there with their eyes fixed on him. They then start to make these very soft, but troubled calls and appear to be anxious and unsettled. They don't take their eyes off of Dylan until he ducks into the barn and is gone from their sight."

> **"**To deny animals' emotions is to deny a large part of who these beings are.**"**
>
> —Marc Bekoff, from **Minding Animals: Awareness, Emotions, and Heart**

Phoebe and David: A Lasting Love

When a cow named Phoebe was rescued and brought to Farm Sanctuary in Watkins Glen, New York, she met and adopted David, an aging sheep nearing the end of his life. She treated him like her child, staying with him every waking minute and sleeping curled up next to him every night. She licked him for hours on end, comforting and soothing him. Whenever David had to be taken into another area for medical treatment, Phoebe was

visibly upset. "The second she got him back, you would have thought it was the reunion of the century," exclaims Susie Coston, the sanctuary's national shelter director. "It was the most incredible thing. The two were completely inseparable." When David died, Phoebe bellowed for hours and searched for him frantically. She was never the same after his death. She died a year later. They are buried side by side.

We work together as a community.

ACCORDING TO PROFESSOR DONALD BROOM, cows, as well as other animals living in herds, abide by "moral codes." They often take actions that benefit the whole group and are helpful to others but of no immediate benefit to themselves. "Just watching them," comments Broom, "we see how they are friendly and altruistic toward each other."

When cows groom one another, it is thought to have many beneficial effects, including minimizing tension and increasing bonding and relationships. When cows know each other well, they will groom one another longer and more frequently. Grooming is often reciprocal; this is thought to be an indication of cows' consideration of and altruistic feelings toward one another.

Cows also work together as a group to "calf-sit." Researchers have frequently observed one or two cows in a field watching over a group of twenty or so calves. In the distance, thirty to forty cows can be spotted grazing or spending time in the water. Researchers are looking into whether the same cows do the sitting or if they rotate. According to Rosamund Young, "the job allocation is done democratically and the cows take it in turn."

In efforts to understand how leaders communicate with their herd and coordinate their movements, researchers are looking at the work of Herbert H. T. Prins of the Netherlands. Prins has spent time studying the behavior of African buffalos and found that they make decisions by voting! They travel together in herds of three to four hundred. When they arise from a rest after grazing, the buffalos will be pointing in different directions. Prins has observed that whichever direction the majority of the buffalos are facing is the direction chosen for the next grazing.

"Living within a group requires a moral code of behavior. . . . Most animals that live in communities exhibit similar moral codes to humans."

—Donald M. Broom, professor of animal welfare, Cambridge University

Helen: Her Love Knows No Bounds

Helen, a Hereford cow, was born blind on a beef production farm. The owner's daughter pleaded with her father to save Helen's life, and she was brought to live at the Catskill Animal Sanctuary in Saugerties, New York. "When Helen arrived she was in an absolute panic," comments Kathy Stevens, founder of the sanctuary and author of *Where the Blind Horse Sings*. "It was a new place, new people, and she couldn't see anything." There was a small steer named Rudy at the sanctuary, who kept to himself. Stevens decided to put Helen and Rudy together. "At first, Rudy retreated. But it took all of a day and a half for them to bond," continues Stevens. "Rudy became Helen's seeing-eye steer. Now Helen's fear is utterly gone.

She knows exactly where the trees are, where to stop, and she can run around the grounds with freedom and joy like a sighted calf. Every blind animal we ever had loves to touch and be touched. Helen will lick you from neck to forehead over and over and over again." Helen also grooms Rudy and Andy, a special-needs horse, with her cow licks. Andy was so severely starved that his growth was stunted and he is still too weak to be with the other horses. He goes out with Rudy and Helen every day and sleeps with them at night in their bed of hay. "Helen is remarkably affectionate," comments Stevens. "She will stand by the gate and bellow to me until I come out. And all she wants is to love and to be touched and petted."

We choose our leaders based on brains, not brawn.

IN A STUDY LED BY Bertrand Dumont of INRA, the French National Institute for Agricultural Research, it was discovered that the qualities that determine which cows become the leaders in a herd are not dominance and strength, but rather such qualities as intelligence, inquisitiveness, and confidence. Bullying and size are not criteria for bovine leadership.

Derek Bailey is also studying leadership in cows, and he points out that the same cows are usually in the front of the herd. He concurs that the leaders are the less dominant ones. Bailey's findings, along with those of Tim Del-Curto of Oregon State University, show that older cows are often selected as leaders, an indication of recognition of the value of experience. For example, they have more knowledge of where food can be found and other information important for survival.

According to Bailey, "Leaders are confident about what they know. Cows will follow an animal that looks like it knows where it's going. Unlike our politicians, there are no debates or expensive campaigning. It's the knowledge that makes the leader."

"For us, the animals are understood to be our equals. They are still our teachers. They are our helpers and our healers. They have been our guardians and we have been theirs. . . . We have deep obligations to them. Without the other animals, we are made less."

—Linda Hogen, novelist

78

I've been known to hold a grudge.

COWS ARE VERY SENSITIVE TO HOW THEY ARE TREATED and will withdraw from humans, as well as other cows, who have treated them unkindly. Researchers have found that cows will approach people who have handled them gently much more frequently than those who have handled them more aggressively. Jeffrey Rushen, research scientist at Agriculture and Agri-Food Canada, discovered that cows' milk production is also affected by the kind of treatment they receive. Rushen and his colleagues demonstrated that when spoken to or handled gently, cows produce significantly more milk than when treated gruffly. They also found that just the presence of a human of whom a cow is frightened lowers milk production by 10 percent. Edmund Pajor, associate professor of animal behavior and welfare at Purdue University, discovered that cows are as sensitive to yelling and hollering as they are to rough physical handling. Conversely, gentle and early handling by humans can reduce fearfulness. Human contact can also be a source of pleasure for cows, who often seek out interaction with humans.

"In ways that matter, we are all the same. I have yet to find an emotion that is normally attributed to humans that is not displayed by animals. Just because they don't speak our words doesn't mean they are not communicating. They are constantly communicating. Once you click in, you can see it. If we let go of the unconscious limits we normally impose on animals and simply look at them, listen to them, and pay attention, they have a whole lot to say, and they say it clearly."

—Kathy Stevens, founder, Catskill Animal Sanctuary

> "Animals are in the world, aware of the world, aware of what happens to them; moreover, what happens to them matters, whether to their body, their freedom, or their life."
>
> —Tom Regan, animal rights activist

Forgive and Forget-not

Maya, a gentle black-and-white cow, lives at Farm Sanctuary in Watkins Glen, New York. Never having had the chance to raise her own calves,

she welcomes and nurtures all the new calves who arrive at the sanctuary. When adoptive families were found for the group of calves she was mothering, Gene Baur, the sanctuary co-founder and one of the country's foremost advocates for animals, had the job of escorting them away from Maya and off to their new homes. According to Baur, Maya was inconsolable, rolling on her back and wailing. To this day, almost fifteen years later, she has not forgiven Gene and will not allow him to come anywhere near her. If he tries to approach her, Maya will charge him.

Farewell to Debbie

When Debbie, a cow who had been rescued by the Woodstock Farm Animal Sanctuary, fell down ill, the other cows at the sanctuary formed a circle around her and mooed and bellowed until a staff member arrived. Sadly, the vet determined that Debbie's arthritis was crippling and that it would be best to put her to sleep. "We dug a grave for Debbie, and when she was laying there all the cows came and gathered around her and just cried and mooed," relays Jenny Brown, the sanctuary's co-founder. "They were so distressed. And when we put her in the grave, they went and lay down on it. Then the whole group went off together somewhere on our four hundred acres and didn't come back for grains for two days. I never expected a reaction like this. I had no idea they were so aware of each other and so bonded."

"When it comes to the ultimate test of what distinguishes humans from the other creatures, scientists have long believed that mourning for the dead represents the real divide."

—Jeremy Rifkin, president, Foundation on Economic Trends

I feel your pain.

RESEARCH BY DR. ALAIN BOISSY and his colleagues at INRA demonstrated that cows are sensitive to and affected by one another's emotional states. For example, they found that it takes cows longer to learn new tasks if they are with a cow that is stressed than when they are with one who is not. They also tend to eat less when their friends are upset.

Empathy had been thought to be unique to humans, although Darwin spoke about animals being empathic in 1871 in his book, *The Descent of Man*. Cows actually show their support and concern for other cows by standing near them during a conflict with another cow and grooming them afterward.

"Animals are conscious of the present and can anticipate the future. They are aware of themselves and of the environment. They know when they are comfortable or uncomfortable. They seem to be able to perceive pain the way we do. If you look at their brains, they are not that different from ours."

—Katherine Haupt, professor of animal behavior, College of Veterinary Medicine, Cornell University

My Love for You Prevails

A two-year-old cow and her young calf were sold at market to two different farms. In the middle of the night, the mother cow broke down a fence and walked seven miles in an unfamiliar area to the farm where her calf had been sold. She was found the next morning, contentedly nursing her calf, who was positively identified by the auction sticker.

Rosamund Young tells the story of a female cow who gave birth to a stillborn calf and suffered from the delivery. Although weak from medical complications, the cow traveled a substantial distance through many fields in order to find her own mother. The next day, farmers found them together and witnessed the mother soothing and grooming her distraught daughter.

"Is it love? When we see examples of maternal behavior in people, we simply see it as a strong example of the bond we call love. When we see the same kind of behavior in any other mammal, we credit that to evolution and leave out and deny the fact that they might love their offspring, when in fact, I can't see any difference."

—Joseph Stookey, professor of animal behavior,
Western College of Veterinary Medicine, University of Saskatchewan

We love our children.

COWS ARE VERY CONNECTED to their offspring and express extreme distress when they are separated. They call out for their calves and move back and forth rapidly, in an effort to reunite. Separation at an early age also has a dramatic impact on the calves' health and well-being. They tend to eat less and have difficulty settling. They cry out for their mothers in a sound resembling bawling. Their stress levels increase, and they are more reactive and easily alarmed. Research has shown that it is the separation from the mother, not the absence of milk, that is upsetting to the calves. Lack of physical or visual contact with other calves has also been shown to be distressing. As with human babies, when allowed to stay with their mothers, calves tend to be more secure and socially adjusted.

CHAPTER FOUR

Pigs

C hildren seem to easily recognize and respond to the affable and appealing nature of pigs. Movies such as *Babe* and *Charlotte's Web* have bolstered the public image of pigs by celebrating their heroic and caring acts. While the intelligence of pigs is gaining recognition, the emotional and social nature of these soft-nosed creatures is less well known. Piglets love to play with and be in the company of familiar piglets and become distressed when they are separated from them.

I am very teachable.

PIGS ARE EXTREMELY INTELLIGENT and are able to respond to verbal communication. Piglets living with humans learn their own names quickly and carry out simple voice commands. The research of Candace Croney, animal behavior bioethicist in the Department of Animal Sciences at Oregon State University, shows that not only can pigs identify and fetch objects upon request, they can understand and respond to commands that involve an action with an object, such as "Push the dumbbell onto the mat." They can even identify the same objects three years later!

Croney showed that when presented with a variety of objects, pigs are able to make comparisons and grasp the relationship between those objects based on color, odor, or location. If there are five blue pots and one green pot, for example, a pig can pick out the green one as being different and could do the same based on odor. They can find the difference no matter where the objects are located and are able to disregard irrelevant information. Surprisingly, they can do all of this without being given any instruction, but simply by being told, "Figure out what you are supposed to do."

I can get it the first time.

PIGS ARE HIGHLY MOTIVATED and extremely persistent. According to Suzanne Held, research fellow at Farm Animal Science at Bristol University, "Pigs will have a go at something and work at it until they get a result. People had thought that only animals with a big cortex learn well and are capable of complex social behavior. But pigs have small brains, and are still fast at learning." Unlike some animals who require practice to learn a new task, pigs are capable of what is known as *one-trial learning*. If they push a lever to the right with their snout and are rewarded with food, for example, they understand in that one try that that particular behavior will have a favorable result and continue to repeat it.

"Pigs are arguably smarter than dogs."

—Bernard E. Rollins, distinguished professor, Colorado State University

Believe it or not, I am high tech!

DR. STANLEY CURTIS, adjunct professor of animal science at the University of Illinois, Urbana, is one of the pioneers of pig cognition. He conducted research with Candace Croney at Pennsylvania State University that demonstrated that pigs can be taught to play video games on the computer! Using their snouts, the pigs learned to move a joystick that directed the cursor to hit targets on the screen. This meant that the pigs were able to grasp that what they were doing in one place had an impact somewhere else. This is a surprisingly complex concept for a non-human animal to understand.

The pigs were also able to retain what they had learned. Croney brought two of the "micro pigs" to the University of Maryland a year later and put them back on the tasks on the computer. "They were a little rusty for the first few minutes," comments Croney. "However, despite being in a new location with the equipment set up somewhat differently from what they had been used to, within one thirty-minute session, they were performing the task as they had in the past."

Croney confides that ten years ago, "if you told people that you were going to study cognition in the pig or the chicken, they looked at you as if you had lost your mind. When Stan talked about putting pigs on the computer, we all laughed at him. Stan put himself on the line as a scientist. He asked, 'Can we use our scientific knowledge as it is to ask the animals how they feel and let them tell us what their experiences and feelings are?' We thought he was crazy. Now it's more acceptable. Working with Stan changed my perspective on pigs."

Forkie and Pinkie: Pigs in the House

Helen Bransford, a pig enthusiast and the illustrator of and inspiration for Jimmy Buffett's book *Swine Not?*, has two beloved pigs she considers part of the family. Forkie and Pinkie, thirteen and one respectively, sleep on the living room sofa and spend a lot of time cuddling. In contrast to their reputa-tion, like all pigs, when given the choice, they are extremely clean creatures.

"They are shockingly intelligent and have a natural affinity for humans," beams Bransford. "As piglets, their favorite thing is to curl up next to you for a warm nap. Well, no, their favorite thing would be food—then human affection. They're very similar to us. Remember, the first transplanted heart was a pig's. And cloned pigs have been designated the best source of multiple organs for transplants in the future.

"Just watch a pig's eyes if you can," continues Bransford, "They know exactly what's going on.

Forkie will come when called, sit, kiss, kneel, play the toy piano, and open the fridge if she gets half a chance. You can teach them just about anything they're physically capable of doing. Forkie's a bit of a diva. She'll sometimes refuse to give visitors her place on the sofa—and if they somehow take it while she's away, she'll remove them with her snout. A snout, by the way, that can smell six feet below ground as well as a single Tic Tac in the bottom of your suitcase.

"With their level of intelligence, pigs can get bored easily, so they need to have toys and things or places to explore—at the very least a rooting box. They love their toys. And I swear, you can see a pig smile—a happy pig just radiates contentment. They're considered the most intelligent animal after primates and dolphins, but pigs as a species have barely been studied at all. I bet that's going to change."

I can see what you see.

MIKE MENDL, PROFESSOR of animal behavior and welfare at Bristol University, and Suzanne Held have been conducting research into a pig's capacity to understand another pig. They have found that pigs might be able to tell what other pigs are thinking. With their colleague Richard Byrne of St. Andrews University, they set up an experiment in which they blocked a subject pig's view of where food was being placed. On either side of the pig were two companion pigs, one whose view was also blocked and one who had a clear view of the food. The subject pig was not able to see what the other pigs could see. When the researchers removed the barriers and the companion pigs were released, the subject pig did, in fact, follow the companion pig who had seen where the food was placed rather than the one who had not. The study suggests that it is possible that a pig can understand what another pig sees. This is referred to as *visual perspective taking* and is an indication of complex cognition.

We know where we stand.

PIGS MIGHT ALSO HAVE the capacity to assess another pig's competitive abilities, recognize who is the more dominant, and adjust their behavior accordingly. Suzanne Held discovered that one pig might be able to recognize when another pig has knowledge of where food is located. The "informed" pig, upon realizing that it's been "found out," will attempt to safeguard the food from the other pig. It might avoid going to the food site when the other pig is near, or eat only if it knows it is alone. Held and Mendl are not certain whether these behaviors represent a pig's ability to deliberately mislead or deceive another pig and conceal knowledge or if they are based on their quickly learning that they will yield rewards. "It is possible that the subordinate pigs actually understood what the dominants could and could not see and adjusted their behavior accordingly, which would show the pig's understanding of the behavior and intentions of others to be a lot more complex than previously assumed," comments Mendl. It has been observed by Mendl and others that pigs, who wear collars that indicate how much food they should receive from an automatic feeder, will pick up collars that have fallen off other pigs and use them to receive another portion of food for themselves. Jonathan Balcolmbe describes this as "a pig's way of hacking into someone else's computer system."

"We haven't even begun to examine the capabilities of pigs. We will find that they are much more complex and clever than we have previously given them credit for. I think that is probably true for lots of animals."

—Ed Pajor, PhD, associate professor,
Animal Behavior and Welfare, Purdue University

Bruce and Aloha: Into the Sunset

Bruce, an older pig who had been badly abused and neglected, was rescued by Animal Place, a farm sanctuary in Vacaville, California. Severely malnourished, he was skin and bones, and for the first month, the staff kept him in the barn just to feed him and help him learn that he could count on being fed every day.

Over time, Bruce gained more than one hundred pounds. He also gained the ability to trust. "It took time before I could pet him," comments Kim Sterla, the co-founder of the sanctuary. "It was more than a year before I could give him a belly rub. But today he is no longer fearful of the people he knows." Bruce also gained a partner, a pig named Aloha. According to Sterla, Bruce and Aloha are very close and sleep together every night. Bruce lies down and is ready for sleep right away. Aloha is very fussy and gets up and down for forty-five minutes or so before she gets comfortable. "It is so precious to watch their relationship evolve," beams Sterla. "They have a routine where they nap under one part of the barn, and then, as the sun sets, waddle off together for the evening. Often Aloha stops to do her business. Bruce always waits for her to catch up. It doesn't get much better than seeing Bruce fat, warm, free, happy, and grazing in peace."

We are at our best when with our friends.

PIGS, LIKE OTHER FARM ANIMALS, are extremely social and form close bonds with one another. They are thought to recognize and remember up to twenty to thirty other pigs. They are very affectionate and greet one another enthusiastically, often grunting and rubbing snouts. Given the opportunity, they seek out and enjoy touch and close physical contact and like to sleep together, often doing so snout to snout.

It is important for pigs to be with others pigs with whom they are familiar. Research shows that they are less stressed by unexpected or challenging events when they are with a "friend." For example, if pigs don't receive a food reward that they were expecting, they become less frustrated if they are with a pig they know. If they are with an unfamiliar pig, however, they often behave more aggressively.

Researchers agree that it is important not to isolate pigs and have found that they suffer when they are alone. "If you are trying to teach pigs something," says Suzanne Held, "you would never take them away from their group abruptly. You have to wean them away if you are going to expose them to a new situation." Pigs who have been raised alone tend to be less playful and more avoidant of new experiences than pigs who have been raised with other pigs. Research by Francoise Wemelsfelder, Ed Pajor, and others has shown that if pigs are isolated or kept from playing with their friends, they behave in ways that indicate depression.

Being with friends also affects pigs' ability to learn, as does their environment. Ian Sneddon, senior lecturer at Queen's University Belfast, and his colleagues found that pigs who are raised with other pigs and in pens that have straw flooring will learn better than those raised alone and in a barren environment. Held points out that, just as with human infants, growing up in a stimulating environment enhances pigs' brain development and enables them, if given the opportunity, to better cope with challenges.

"Pigs develop close relationships, particularly if they have grown up together. If they have the opportunity to mature together, the bond pretty much lasts a lifetime. They will make choices to be with one another—to sleep together, take mud baths together, and roam together. They become partners."

—Kim Sterla, co-founder, Animal Place

Hope and Johnny: Loyal and Loving

Hope and Johnny, two pigs who lived at Farm Sanctuary in Orland, California, had an extremely close friendship. Hope had an injured leg and was unable to walk. Johnny, who was much younger, would stay by her when she ate to keep other pigs from bothering her and would remain by her side throughout the day. He would also sleep with her at night, keeping her warm. Hope died of old age, and Johnny, who was healthy at the time, appeared devastated. He died several weeks later of no known cause.

I am very sensitive.

PIGS ARE EXTREMELY SENSITIVE to what goes on around them as well as to their environment. They are easily stressed and just being weighed can be a source of great anxiety. Being placed with unfamiliar pigs can cause extreme tension and fear. Rough handling is also stressful and can affect a pig's behavior, growth, and reproduction. Paul Hemsworth, professor of animal welfare and behavior at University of Melbourne, has shown that if pigs are mistreated, they are two and a half times less likely to become pregnant. As with humans, stress also affects a pig's cognitive ability. Mike Mendl demonstrated that if pigs are exposed to stressful situations, they make more errors or take longer to perform a task.

"Careful scientific research is validating what we intuitively understand: that animals feel, and their emotions are as important to them as ours are to us. Animals' emotions are . . . raw and uncontrolled. Their joy is the purest and most contagious of joys, and their grief the deepest and most devastating.

When animals express their feelings they pour out like water from a spout. Indeed, when we pay attention, animals display a mindful presence, unfiltered emotions, and a zest for life. . . . Their passions bring us to our knees in delight and sorrow."

—Marc Bekoff, from **The Emotional Lives of Animals**

Pigs are able to communicate their anxiety. In a study conducted in London, researchers taught pigs to press one lever when they felt normal and another when they felt anxious. Not only could the pigs distinguish their emotional states, they were also able to retain what they had learned. In response to a stressful event at a later date, they were able to again press the appropriate lever to convey their anxiety.

We are easy to read.

FRANCOISE WEMELSFELDER and her colleagues demonstrated that people could accurately judge animals' emotions through observation.

They assembled groups of people with no previous experience interpreting animal expressions and asked them to observe a number of animals, mostly pigs, interact with a human. They then asked them to write down adjectives that best described the pigs' expressions.

"Whether observers were students, scientists, pig farmers, veterinarians, or animal rights activists," noted Wemelsfelder, "we persistently found high levels of agreement in how they judged the pigs. In their own words, observers created coherent and meaningful descriptive language that they could use to characterize the expression of individual pigs in precise and repeatable ways."

Winnie and Buster:
A Story of Loss and Recovery

Winnie and Buster were rescued by Farm Sanctuary in Watkins Glen, New York, when they were piglets. After five years of being together constantly, Buster was injured and eventually had to be put to sleep. Afterward, Winnie kept to herself, sleeping alone rolled up in a little ball. She didn't want to be touched and made no attempt to make new friends. The staff was very concerned, as Winnie seemed to have given up. She lost a great deal of weight, but tests revealed that nothing was wrong physically.

Two years later, the sanctuary adopted a new group of piglets and, according to national shelter director Susie Coston, "Winnie became a whole new pig. Now she's the boss of the herd, running around with the piglets, playing games, and spinning. She is finally letting herself care about another animal again." Winnie is attached to the piglets, staying with them during the day and sleeping with them at night. "This group woke Winnie up and brought her back to life," comments Coston. "She's like she was with Buster."

More recently, Professor Wemelsfelder has asked people to observe pigs in different housing environments. When the pigs are housed in healthy, stimulating environments, some words used to describe the pigs are "friendly, curious, lively, content, playful, confident." When they are kept in small, dark, barren pins, the pigs are perceived as "timid, anxious, bored, frustrated, or helpless."

We know what we want and need . . . and can tell you!

PIGS CAN LEARN TO PERFORM BEHAVIORS that communicate what their preferences are, such as how much heat or light they would like to have in their environment. Researchers are working to see things from a pig's point of view to best understand their needs and make recommendations as to how to meet them. They are asking, for example, whether it is more important to be with other pigs or to build a nest, or whether food is more important than socializing. One way of finding out is by giving pigs options and observing their choices. "We can learn a lot about animals by what animals have to tell us," comments Ed Pajor. "The fact that they have preferences and can demonstrate them to us represents the idea that animals are capable of making choices. Paying attention to their vocalizations, to their behavior, the way they move, the way they turn their heads, the way they approach us or avoid us are all important in terms of understanding them." Professor Stan Curtis of the University of Illinois, Urbana, is actually hoping to teach pigs a crude language in order to learn more about what they feel and enable them to communicate their needs.

"This is the larger lesson of animal cognition research: It humbles us. We are not alone in our ability to invent or plan."

—Virginia Morell in **National Geographic**

We need to play.

PLAY IS THOUGHT TO BE extremely important to an animal's development and an indication of their complex capacities. According to Compassion in World Farming, "play develops cognitive skills necessary for behavioral adaptability, flexibility, inventiveness, and versatility." Being able to explore and play with toys is essential to pigs. Young pigs love to play fight, nip and chase one another, and play in water. When pigs are provided with pens that are roomy and have peat flooring with straw, they play ten times as long as when they are in pens that are barren. Researchers at Bristol University showed that piglets who have had no toys to play with are extremely timid, and if a new person enters their space, they huddle in a corner and freeze. In contrast, pigs who have had things to play with are less timid and will approach the person.

Researchers are concluding that play feels good and provides pigs and other animals with a sense of pleasure. When animals are playing, researchers have found that the chemicals in the brain that indicate pleasure and excitement are released. Without the opportunity to play, pigs can become bored, lethargic, and even depressed.

"I think all animals are sentient in different ways, with different types of experience. One type isn't better than another type. We all fit into the web of life in our own way. As a society, I think we are ready to accept animals as fellow sentient beings. Talking about animals as sentient is compatible with and can be perfectly good science."

—Francoise Wemelsfelder, behavioral scientist, Scottish Agricultural College

She's Not Heavy, She's My Sister

In Jenny Campbell's book *Animals are Smarter than Jack*, Lesley Franklin tells the story of her two pet pigs, sisters Bacon and Eggs. One day Bacon disappeared. Franklin searched for her but was unable to find her. Eggs, however, still showed up for dinner every evening. Franklin continued to search for Bacon and eventually found her not far from home. She was pinned under the branch of a tree. Surrounding Bacon was a nest of fresh grass for her to eat. Franklin believes that the grass had been placed there by Eggs, whose efforts saved Bacon's life.

All Together Again

When more than one hundred pigs were found badly neglected on a farm in Olean, New York, Farm Sanctuary in Watkins Glen, New York, brought more than fifty of the littlest ones to their sanctuary and found homes for many of the others. One mother pig named Susie was taken to a foster home with her four piglets, Cameron, Carmen, Cody, and Calvin. There the piglets were separated from Susie, who weighed more than five hundred pounds, for fear that she would hurt them in an enclosed space. Permanent homes were then found for the four piglets in Texas with Brooke Chavez, who luckily sent for Susie soon after. When Susie first arrived, Brooke planned to keep her separate from her piglets. By this time Susie weighed eight hundred pounds and had been acting very aggressively, which is common for pigs when separated from their offspring. When Brooke went to feed the new piglets the day after Susie arrived, they were nowhere to be seen. Brooke quickly looked into Susie's pen where she found mother and babies cuddled together sleeping peacefully. Susie and her piglets have been inseparable ever since.

> **"The more we learn about farm animals, the more we are understanding how similar humans are to other animals. We are all shaped by our experiences and memories, both good and bad, communicate through various means, and develop complex relationships with others in a social system."**
>
> —Gene Baur, president and co-founder, Farm Sanctuary

We need our mothers.

IN NATURE, weaning is a gradual process. Piglets remain with or close to their mothers until they are ready to be on their own. Today, on most farms, piglets are removed from their mothers as early as three to four weeks of age, and sometimes earlier, at a time when they are still dependent on and attached to her. This abrupt weaning is extremely challenging for the piglets and has many negative affects. Dan Weary and David Fraser of University of British Columbia have found that piglets begin to cry out immediately upon separation. The younger they are when they are weaned, the more frequently they will cry and the higher the pitch will be. Pigs that are weaned abruptly usually eat less and begin to lose weight. They also tend to demonstrate more aggression, recklessness, and abnormal behavior. Adroaldo Zanella of Norway has shown that piglets that are weaned at an early age perform worse on memory tests. It appears that if piglets are mixed with other piglets prior to being weaned, they have a better response to separation. They fight less, seem less stressed, and learn social skills more quickly.

Abrupt weaning is also stressful for the sow. Ed Pajor and his colleagues have demonstrated that separation is more upsetting if the sow has been removed from her nest. They recorded and played back the vocalizations of a sow's piglets, and found that her response was more intense when outside the nest. According to Pajor, when hearing their cries, "the sow got up and ran toward the speaker and started vocalizing loudly to call her piglets and let them know where she was." When she was allowed to stay in her nest, she appeared less distressed. Sows recognize the calls of their own piglets and can identify and respond rapidly to a cry of need.

"Even if pigs are kept from each other, they will sleep nose to nose through a fence, because they are so upset about not being able to be with each other. They are much more aware than we think. We don't take animals to the vet without another animal because they are absolutely devastated. Pigs mourn themselves to death; all these animals do."

—Susie Coston, national shelter director, Farm Sanctuary

Sending Out an SOS

When JoAnn Altsman suffered a heart attack, her dog, Bear, barked, and her pig, Lulu, squeezed her body under a dog door. Scraped and bleeding, Lulu laid herself in the middle of traffic until she attracted help. Intermittently, she ran into the house, apparently to check on Mrs. Altsman. Lulu's efforts led to recovery for Mrs. Altsman and fame for herself. Her heroism is included in the book *Beasts: True Stories of Animals Who Choose to Do Good*.

CHAPTER FIVE

Sheep and Goats

These wooly creatures melt the hearts of those lucky enough to spend time with them. It is interesting that sheep, who have such fascinating faces, are so observant of and responsive to the faces of others, in much the same way humans are. Research is now uncovering amazing similarities in how the sheep brain and the human brain process visual information. Goats are naturally curious, inquisitive, and playful. Their warm, friendly personalities speak volumes, showing us their unique and engaging essence.

We like to be connected.

RESEARCH SHOWS that being separated from their flock produces anxiety in sheep. When isolated, their heart rates increase, their stress hormones become elevated, they bleat more frequently, and the part of their brain that controls fear and anxiety exhibits increased activity. Being separated from their flock also affects a sheep's eating and drinking. They have more difficulty digesting their food, and they drink less water. Sheep who are isolated become restless and unable to soothe and settle.

The bonds sheep form among themselves help them manage the environment and cope with stressful events. Similar to cows' grooming one another, sheep rub heads with each other and make cheek-to-cheek contact, which is thought to strengthen their relationships and reduce tension.

When with their flock, sheep are more relaxed and less vigilant. They are also more adventurous. Alain Boissy and Bertrand Dumont studied the impact of being with familiar sheep. They found that when lambs are with others they know, they are more likely to try novel foods or move to new feeding sites. When they are with unfamiliar animals, they stick to their established food preferences.

"I have discovered that the flock is a powerful social unit rather than a bunch of mindless followers. . . . Sheep have no defense against predators except escape and safety in numbers, so their response makes sense. I have seen many instances of the members of the flock watching out for each other and accommodating a member who is hurt or ill."

—Stephanie Marohn, from **The Way of the Sheep**

"After more than seven decades of cumulative discoveries about . . . consciousness, we have not yet found any fundamental differences between humans and mammals."

—Bernard Baars, former senior research fellow, Neurosciences Institute of San Diego

The sight of you soothes my soul.

KEITH KENDRICK, professor of cognitive and behavioral neuroscience at the Babraham Institute near Cambridge, found that when sheep are suffering from separation anxiety, seeing photographs of the faces of a familiar breed of sheep can reduce their stress. "Sheep are much like us in that they recognize each other's faces in photographs," comments Kendrick. "They have the same specialized part of the brain as humans do to help them recognize and remember faces."

Professor Kendrick and his colleagues found that when sheep were taken to a room and isolated from their flock, their heart rates and stress hormone levels were elevated, they made protest bleats, and they moved around with increased frequency. When shown photographs of inverted triangles resembling the shape of a sheep's face, or photographs of unfamiliar goat's faces, their stress levels remained elevated. However, when shown photographs of sheep from their flock, behavioral and physiological signs of stress were significantly reduced.

Kendrick believes that providing photos or videos of other sheep could be an effective method for helping sheep manage their separation anxiety. "A sheep being soothed by seeing pictures of familiar sheep," comments Kendrick, "can be compared to our carrying photos of loved ones in our wallets or handbags."

I can read you like a book.

NOT ONLY CAN SHEEP be calmed by seeing photographs of the faces of a familiar breed of sheep, they can also read and respond to emotional cues from both human and sheep faces. Professor Keith Kendrick's work shows that sheep react to facial expressions and prefer a human face that is smiling to one that shows anger, and a calm, contented sheep face to a stressed and anxious one.

When sheep are faced with pictures of smiling or angry versions of the same human face or of calm or anxious versions of the same sheep face, and are given a food reward for whichever they choose, they will select the smiling human or the calm sheep. They appear to deliberately avoid angry or anxious faces even when they are associated with food.

"This does open up the possibility that sheep have much richer social and emotional lives than we would give them credit for," comments Kendrick. "They would not have developed these recognition skills unless they needed to use them in their everyday lives." Kendrick also believes that "if sheep can do this then the likelihood is that many other species can, too."

You are always on my mind.

SHEEP HAVE BEEN SHOWN TO RECOGNIZE at least fifty different individual sheep and ten different humans by their faces, although according to Professor Kendrick, they can probably recognize far more than this. They can also remember these faces even when they have not seen them for two years or more.

When images of two sheep or human faces are "morphed" on a computer so that they are made progressively more identical, sheep can distinguish the two faces when there is as little as 5–10 percent difference. This means that sheep can pick up on even the most subtle differences in facial appearance and detect details, just as humans can.

Kendrick's research with Claude Fabre-Nys and several other colleagues shows that female sheep found the faces of some male sheep more attractive than others. The areas of the brain governing emotional responses became activated when they saw the faces of males they preferred. They also found that females were more interested in older rather than younger males. Even more amazing, male sheep were found to prefer mates that resembled their mothers!

Kendrick posed the question that, while sheep can recognize and remember individuals, are they able to visualize and think about friends in their absence? His work has attempted to find evidence that they can form and use mental images of faces in the same way humans do. For example, he found that they are able from just seeing the frontal view of a face to recognize that same individual in profile, suggesting they may be able to perform *mental rotation*, which means they can turn images around in their head. In some studies sheep were put in situations where familiar faces of friends were expected or cued in some way but were not actually there. Just as with the human brain, the same part of the brain responding to the actual sight of these faces became activated. While it is difficult to prove that sheep, or any other animal, can picture and experience feelings about individuals in their absence, evidence so far does suggest that they probably can.

Kendrick has concluded from his studies that sheep have "a far greater level of social awareness and emotional complexity than we had previously thought."

"The way emotions are expressed in humans and animals are universal and not learned."

—Paul Ekman, from **Emotions Inside Out**

We Can Out-sheep You!

The Guardian newspaper in London reported a story about a flock of sheep in northern England who discovered a way to get over supposedly hoof-proof metal grids. The grids were installed to prevent the determined sheep from entering and eating from local gardens in the town of Marsden. Dorothy Linden, a local resident, told the paper, "I've seen them doing it, and they're very clever. They lie down on their side, or sometimes on their back, and roll over the metal grids until they are clear." Alternate plans to protect the gardens were being sought.

We can anticipate events.

RESEARCHERS AT BRISTOL UNIVERSITY have shown that sheep form expectations of what is likely to occur. For example, if grazing in a field, they generally ignore passing traffic. However, when the car that delivers their food arrives, they run toward it enthusiastically. Like cows, sheep also know when the grasses in a field will be replenished and wait until that time to return to graze. Lambs have the capacity to determine and select over time those foods that will provide them with the most energy.

Wildlife scientist Valerius Geist performed an experiment with a group of sheep to whom he regularly brought treats of salt. On one of his visits, instead of giving them the salt immediately, he disappeared with it behind some shrubbery. Rather than look for him at the point at which he disappeared, the sheep estimated the point at which he would have come out of hiding had he continued walking in a straight line, and they waited for him there.

"It is surprisingly easy to recognize basic or primary emotions in animals. All we have to do is look, listen, and smell. Their faces, their eyes, and the ways in which they carry themselves can be used to make strong inferences about what they are feeling. Changes in muscle tone, posture, gait, facial expression, eye size and gaze, vocalizations, and odors, singly and together, all indicate emotional responses to certain situations. A person doesn't even need to be consciously aware of these aspects; from simply watching an animal, people can often intuitively sense the correct emotion."

—Marc Bekoff, from **The Emotional Lives of Animals**

Hannah and Rambo: A Heart Restored

Hannah, a sheep found wandering in a Queens, New York, cemetery, was brought to the Catskill Animal Sanctuary. Initially, Hannah was quarantined in a separate stall for a period of adjustment. Whenever the staff went in to see her, Hannah would leap up the walls trying to get away. "She had never known any kindness from humans," comments Kathy Stevens, the founder of the sanctuary. Stevens and her staff took turns patiently sitting with Hannah day after day, being careful not to look her in the eye, which would have been too threatening. Little by little, Hannah started to do better, but she was still overwhelmed by so many humans. "We looked at this broken spirit, and we thought that what she needed was Rambo," continues Stevens.

A ram who had long resided at the sanctuary, Rambo was known for his ability to befriend and help heal the emotional wounds of other animals. Stevens began letting Hannah out of her stall, and very quickly, she became attached to Rambo. In the mornings, she would walk the place frantically, screaming until she found him. She would not let him out of her sight. They'd spend all day side by side until it was time for Hannah to go back to the barn for the evening. "Rambo taught Hannah to trust us. Sheep are instinctively terrified of dogs, who have been their predators. But Hannah comes up to my dog, Murphy, and nibbles him and nuzzles his head," says Stevens. Hannah also developed her maternal side. When Norma Jean, a frightened turkey, arrived at the sanctuary, Hannah mothered and watched out for her. When Norma Jean became agitated or was startled by a pig or a horse, Hannah would go over to her and calm her down. "But on visiting days when lots of people arrive, Hannah still looks to Rambo for reassurance," comments Stevens. "When Rambo walks off, she charges after him."

My voice gives me away.

MARK FEINSTEIN, a professor of cognitive science at Hampshire College in Amherst, Massachusetts, found that the vocal patterns of sheep change when they are isolated from their flock or when their lambs are separated from them. Thought to be unique to human speech, Feinstein has discovered that sheep have the ability to manipulate their vocal chords to make different and specific sounds. They are also capable of distinguishing their lambs' cries even from great distances.

Veterinarian and author James Herriot tells a story that captures his marvel at a sheep's maternal connection to her lambs. He visited a farm where more than two hundred lambs were gathered in a barn for inoculations. They were protesting with high-pitched sounds and their mothers, who were gathered outside the barn, were "baa-ing" deeply and unrelentingly. Herriot couldn't imagine how the sheep and their lambs, who to his eye all looked alike, were going to reunite. He thought it would take hours to sort themselves out and match up. To his amazement, it took twenty-five seconds. The farmers opened the doors, the lambs poured out, and the distraught sheep found their offspring.

We get attached.

SHEEP CAN FORM STRONG ATTACHMENTS to certain people. They express their affection by nuzzling their heads against their human friends. According to Jeffrey Moussaieff Masson, sheep respond when their names are called, just as dogs do. Professor Kendrick has found that sheep can remember specific humans they were close to for more than two years after last seeing them. He also found that the parts of the sheep's brain that process current familiar faces still respond to the faces of friends from the past. According to Kendrick, a number of farmers have reported that upon returning to their sheep after a period of separation, as long as three years in one case, the sheep appeared "depressed." When the sheep saw the farmers, they showed immediate and enthusiastic signs of recognition. Kendrick believes that sheep also have some capacity to think about absent friends and experience an emotional response when they do.

"We [humans] are obviously capable of both recognizing faces of people when we meet them and thinking about them when they are not around using a similar specialized part of the brain as is present in the sheep," comments Kendrick. "Therefore it would be surprising if sheep were not also capable of thinking 'consciously' about absent individuals using this same system."

 136

"To my mind, the life of a lamb is no less precious than that of a human being."

—Gandhi

Wooly: The Sheep Who Thought He Was a Horse

Wooly was rescued from a Pennsylvania horse farm by the Humane Society of the United States and brought to the Poplar Spring Animal Sanctuary. He had originally come from a petting zoo, but was given away because he wasn't friendly enough with the children. The farm owner kept Wooly with the horses and did not give him much attention. He was extremely thin, matted, unshorn, and terrified of people.

The staff first kept Wooly isolated until he was vaccinated, had recovered from some ailments, and had gained some weight. When he was ready to be with other animals, they decided to let him stay with the horses rather than the other sheep. They had observed him calling out to the horses and guessed that he must have bonded with them at his previous residence.

When they let him out of his yard, he ran directly to Darcy, the largest horse, and stood under his legs, appearing extremely content. From that day on, Wooly became one of the herd, never letting the horses out of his sight. Wherever the horses wandered, little Wooly would trot along with his short, stumpy legs.

The staff at the sanctuary thought Wooly might be better off with the sheep, because he seemed so exhausted from trying to keep up with the horses. But Wooly took one look at the sheep and ran the other way. Eventually, Wooly became more relaxed with the sheep and even displayed an interest in a female sheep named Greta.

Today, Wooly spends his days with Greta and the other rescued sheep. He has also learned to trust people.

> **"We must look at animals as whole, integrated beings from the start. A holistic approach gives a far richer picture of how capable animals are of feeling, how much they feel, and how rich their emotional repertoire is."**
>
> —Francoise Wemelsfelder, senior scientist, Scottish Agricultural College

I'm not just one of the herd.

RESEARCH HAS RECENTLY SHOWN that animals have personalities. In 1996, Dr. Sam Gosling, a psychology professor and researcher at the University of Texas at Austin and founder of the Personality Institute, conducted a pioneering study with his colleagues to explore this possibility. Skeptical at first, they were surprised by what they discovered. "Every way you measure it, and we have measured it a bunch of ways, it shows that animals have personalities. Actually, it would be unusual if evolution gave only us personality as we diverged from animals." Gosling believes that one of the reasons that the prevailing thinking was that animals didn't have personalities is that "we didn't know how to look for it." Currently, many researchers are devising numerous studies in this area. They have even found that squid, trout, and lizards have personalities. Animals behaving and reacting in the same ways repeatedly to the same stimuli is accepted as scientific evidence of personality traits.

Researchers have discovered three different emotional states in dairy sheep: calm, anxious, or somewhere in between. Calm sheep have been found to be more nurturing to their lambs than nervous sheep. They are more available to them, spend more time with them, and return more quickly when their lambs are in need. It is interesting to note that the milk produced by calm animals is of better quality than the milk produced by anxious animals.

Dr. Piet Drent of the Netherlands Institute of Ecology is conducting one of the most comprehensive studies investigating personality in wild animals. He believes that the difference in human and animal personalities is "a matter of degrees, not of differences."

"We cannot escape the conclusion that animals have personality. It is more a question of whether we want to see it or not, whether we are prepared to see it," comments Gosling. "One of the things that is really sort of striking is that I get one of two very different reactions to my work in this field. When I say that animals have personalities and we can measure it, anyone who knows animals or has pets looks at me like I am crazy and says, 'Well of course!' Yet I can say that exact thing to scientists and they will shrug their shoulders, look at me like I'm crazy, and say, 'Of course they don't have personalities.' You get these two beliefs that animals having personalities is obviously right or is obviously wrong. You rarely get anything in the middle."

We like to learn.

GOATS HAVE DEMONSTRATED the ability to recognize and respond differently to different symbols. Researchers N. E. Blakeman and T. H. Friend taught goats to press one panel when the letter "X" was shown on a backdrop and another panel when the letter "O" was shown. Pressing the right lever resulted in receiving food. The goats seemed to have a good time learning. They reportedly ran past the researchers to get to the testing area and wanted to stay behind even after the tests were done.

" . . . animals undoubtedly feel, think, love, hate, will, and even reason."

—David Hume

Olivia and Dylan:
Love Comes in All Shapes and Sizes

Woodstock Farm Animal Sanctuary director Jenny Brown describes Olivia as a goat "full of personality." As a pet goat, she was abandoned when her human family's house burned down. When Olivia arrived at the sanctuary, she was emaciated and her hooves were so overgrown that her legs had become crippled. Brown and her staff soon fattened her up, straightened out her feet, and restored her to health.

"With Olivia everything is on her terms," explains Brown. "She can be very moody. One moment, she loves being loved, and the very next moment, she'll give the message, Don't touch me."

Soon after Olivia's arrival, Dylan, a calf of just five days old, was

brought to the sanctuary by a neighbor who found him tied to a tree, destined to be auctioned. Scrawny and malnourished, Dylan was nursed back to health and put in a pen next to Olivia.

Up until Dylan arrived, Olivia had shown no interest in other animals. When she was put in a pen with other goats, she would hide in the corner. So Olivia was kept in her own pen, but she suddenly seemed interested in her new neighbor. She was seen letting Dylan lick her. When they were put in a pen together, they became inseparable. She was an older goat, much bigger than Dylan. He was a baby who had been taken away from his mother, and he immediately took to Olivia.

During the day they would roam outside together. Brown recalls, "He would run and jump and frolic around her, and she would do the equivalent of rolling her eyes at him and sort of ignore him. But they would stick together. They had something special." They shared a large pen for some time, but then Dylan got too big—1,500 pounds! He didn't know his own size and thought he was still a baby. When his roughhousing got too much for Olivia, who was rather frail, he had to be put in the pasture with the other steer. But during the day, free-roaming Olivia would go over and stand next to Dylan through the fence. She would graze next to him, and he would "moo" for her. They would lie down together, back-to-back, with the fence between them.

Recently, Olivia was diagnosed with lymphoma and is receiving round-the-clock TLC. She is still full of personality, enjoying constant attention, and mowing through trays of wheatgrass every day. Dylan remains the friendliest steer at the sanctuary, often coming up to the fence when his name is called. He has a new goat friend, Jack, whose coat is covered in cow licks, evidence of the daily grooming from his cow-pal Dylan.

"Goats are the animals that most act like dogs. They come right up to you. They seek out your affection. They'll rub against your legs. They fight and bicker amongst themselves and then they make up. They have complex social structures and are very interesting to watch. They're also incredibly affectionate and love attention."

—Jenny Brown, founder, Woodstock Farm Animal Sanctuary

We know how to stay safe.

KIDS, OR BABY GOATS, LEARN which foods agree with them and which don't. They choose to eat the healthy foods and avoid the unhealthy ones. If they are offered both, they can tell the difference and will select the healthy food.

When they are met with people or objects that are unfamiliar to them, kids seek safety by their mothers' sides. They also express their stress by increased vocalizing or shying away.

Albie: A Spirit Unhampered

Albie, a white goat who was found in Prospect Park in Brooklyn, New York, was rescued by the Woodstock Farm Animal Sanctuary. His legs had been tied together tightly, cutting off the circulation and leaving his front left leg badly infected. Jenny Brown, the sanctuary's co-founder, tried to save Albie's leg through antibiotics and by treating the wound with ointments and homeopathic remedies. However, the wound would not heal. In order to save Albie, his leg had to be amputated just above the knee. Jenny had also lost part of her leg as a child due to bone cancer. Her experience enabled her to help Albie. She contacted her prosthetist, Erik J. Tompkins, who had fitted her with her current prosthesis. Tompkins is now doing the same for Albie. Others have stepped up to the plate to help Albie, as well. Martin Rowe, publisher of Lantern Books, ran in the New York City ING marathon and called it the "Run for Albie." He raised $11,000 to help cover the costs of Albie's surgeries. "This is about giving one of our animals a better quality of life, just like you would do for a house pet or a child," comments Brown. "And what we are hoping here is that Albie will walk again on four legs."

Afterword

AMY HATKOFF'S FINE ACCOUNT OF THE EMOTIONAL AND MENTAL capacities of farm animals cannot help but give greater context and meaning to the cause of animal protection, especially given the vast number of animals raised in inhumane confinement conditions on factory farms.

The signature farm animal welfare issue in the 1980s and 1990s was the campaign to halt the mistreatment of young male calves raised for veal. That campaign faltered in legislatures, but it penetrated popular consciousness, with more and more Americans shunning a product that involved the torment of baby animals. More recently, farm animal campaigns have exposed the cruelties of the battery cage and the gestation crate—two similarly inhumane confinement systems.

Our movement is now beginning to gain victories on the broader range of farm animal welfare issues. The first decade of the twenty-first century saw voters in Florida (2002) and Arizona (2006) support a prohibition on the gestation crate, and major pork and veal producers announce phase-outs of crate housing (2007). During the same period, several hundred institutional cafeterias and food purveyors have made the switch to cage-free eggs.

There has been other progress. In 2008, a dramatic investigation of a California slaughtering plant compelled the USDA to ban "downer" cattle from the nation's food supply, and campaigners waged an epic battle to pass Proposition 2 in California, to mandate that animals raised for food be permitted to spread their wings and turn around. Its success will dramatically improve the lives of an estimated 20 million farm animals each year and set a powerful precedent for reform elsewhere.

The people, the ideas, and the individual creatures Amy Hatkoff writes about here have all done so much to make this world a little—no, a lot—better for animals. I'm grateful for all of them, just as I'm grateful for the author's effort to tell their stories.

Wayne Pacelle, President of The Humane Society of the United States

What You Can Do: Creating a More Humane World for Farm Animals

"The greatness of a nation and its moral progress can be judged by the way its animals are being treated."

—Gandhi

HAVING GLIMPSED THE SURPRISINGLY ADVANCED CAPACITIES OF these intelligent, social, and emotional beings, hopefully we will all be moved to take action on their behalf. As we become more aware of their reality, it becomes increasingly difficult to look at and accept how they are being treated. Recognizing their abilities and becoming aware of their sentience may be another "inconvenient truth."

Worldwide, billions of chickens, turkeys, cows, pigs, sheep, goats, and other animals are farmed for our benefit under conditions that are harsh and often inhumane. In the words of Gene Baur, co-founder of the first farm animal sanctuary in the United States, "On farms where animals are raised for food, sentient beings are treated like inanimate commodities. Nameless millions are crammed into cages and crates so tightly that they can't walk, turn around, or even stretch their limbs. They never feel the sun on their backs or have a breath of fresh air, and they never know human kindness."

Government officials are beginning to listen to evidence about the social, emotional, and cognitive abilities of farm animals, as well as their capacity to feel pain and to suffer. Slowly changes are beginning to be implemented. Europe and Australia have made the most advances in terms of protecting farm animals. Through the efforts of Compassion in World Farming along with the European Coalition for Farm Animals, chickens, turkeys, cows, pigs, sheep, goats, and other farm animals are now recognized throughout the European Union as sentient beings by law and are entitled to certain protections.

"Our problem with realizing the full implications of animal sentience may not be the difficulty of 'liberating' animals, but of liberating ourselves from centuries of conditioned thinking. Only then can we see animals for who they are and award them the respect and compassion they deserve."

—Joyce D'Silva, ambassador, Compassion in World Farming

While there are no federal laws in the United States that safeguard animals while they are on the farm, numerous independent polls reveal that federal protection for farm animals is overwhelmingly supported by American citizens. Currently, measures are being taken by several states to begin to improve conditions for farm animals. California, Florida, Arizona, Colorado, and Oregon have banned the use of gestation crates, in which pregnant sows are confined in a space too small to move or turn around. Citizens in Arizona, California, and Colorado voted to ban the use of veal crates, where male calves are placed immediately after birth, tethered by their necks, and fed an inadequate diet for months. In 2008, California became the first state to ban the use of battery cages, in which chickens are unable to move or even spread their wings.

Steps are also being taken by the food industry, corporations, groups, and individuals to reduce cruelty to animals. Famed chef Wolfgang Puck will not purchase veal from producers who crate calves. More than 160 schools in the United States have either ended or greatly reduced their use of battery-cage eggs. Whole Foods Market, Wild Oats, Ben & Jerry's, AOL, Google, Yahoo, and Nike have all reduced or eliminated the use of battery-cage eggs in their stores, products, and cafeterias.

These are important steps toward protecting farm animals and are examples of the growing concern for their well-being. Below are some actions each of us can take to improve their lives in our own communities and beyond.

Contact an advocacy and education organization

There are numerous organizations worldwide working to improve the treatment of farm animals as well as to educate individuals, communities, governments, policy makers, and the agriculture business. They can guide you in campaigning for farm animals and in encouraging officials to improve conditions for animals in your community and nationwide. Contact one of the organizations listed in the resources section (page 162) to find out how you can make a difference.

Spread the word

Many organizations have excellent educational and advocacy materials about farm animals that you can share with your family, friends, classmates, and colleagues. This information can also be used to compose letters to your local newspaper and television or radio stations. Acknowledging the media for reporting on farm animal issues can encourage more coverage.

Support a farm sanctuary

Farm animal sanctuaries offer the opportunity to interact with pigs, cows, sheep, chickens, turkeys, goats, and other farm animals. They conduct tours, and several of them offer workshops and classes, which are often tailored to children, making a visit to a farm sanctuary a wonderful family or school trip. To find a sanctuary in your area, see the sanctuaries listed in this book (page 158) or visit www.farmanimalshelters.org.

By making a donation to a farm sanctuary, you can help cover the costs to house, feed, and provide medical care for an animal. Sponsoring a farm animal makes a meaningful gift for adults, as well as for children. It is an excellent project for school children and provides an opportunity to learn about farm animals and community action. Most sanctuaries will send photographs, information, and reports on the sponsored animal.

Become a conscious consumer

As consumers, we can have an impact on the way animals are treated. Growing numbers of people are choosing to reduce the amount of animal food in their diets or to eliminate it altogether. Many are attempting to purchase products from farms where the wellbeing of animals is considered and practices are less harsh. These products are often referred to as "humanely raised." Several of the organizations in this book can offer guidance in making dietary changes as well as making more conscientious choices.

In addition to the obvious benefits to animals, the health benefits of a vegetarian or vegan diet to humans are being increasingly recognized. These diets are also more beneficial for the environment. Raising farm animals for food generates more greenhouse gas emissions than all the world's vehicles combined. The grains that are used to feed farm animals could instead be used to help alleviate the growing crisis in world hunger.

In their book, *The Ten Trusts: What We Must Do for the Animals We Love*, Jane Goodall and Marc Bekoff tell us, "After all is said and done, silence is betrayal." Let us not remain silent, rather, let us use our voices to speak for and protect those who cannot do so for themselves. Just as the duck in Vancouver pulled on the pant leg of the police officer to help rescue her ducklings, the animals are tugging at our sleeves, asking us to help. Knowledge is power—and with seeing the truth comes responsibility. If we stand together and take action, we can begin to make this world safer for all those with whom we share it.

"Animals are more than ever a test of our character, of mankind's capacity for empathy, and for decent, honorable conduct and faithful stewardship. We are called to treat them with kindness, not because they have rights or power or some claim to equality, but because they don't."

—Matthew Scully, from **Dominion**

Sanctuaries

Sanctuary:
* A sacred place
* A place of refuge or asylum
* A reserved area in which animals are protected
* A consecrated place where sacred objects are kept
* A shelter from danger or hardship

A SANCTUARY OFFERS ANIMALS RESCUED FROM ABUSE OR NEGLECT refuge and provides an opportunity for them to live out their lives as nature intended. It is a place where animals heal, emotionally and physically, and where they learn to trust. At a sanctuary, animals are loved and cherished. They are given and known by their names and seen for the individuals they are. They have the opportunity to develop relationships with their human companions and one another. The animals rescued by sanctuaries represent and carry the hope for and spirit of the billions of farm animals who do not know such safety.

You can visit the following sanctuaries or support them in many ways, including sponsoring an animal. For a more complete list, visit www.farm-animalshelters.org.

Animal Place
17314 McCourtney Road
Grass Valley, CA 95949
707-449-4814
www.animalplace.org

Catskill Animal Sanctuary
316 Old Stage Road
Saugerties, NY 12477
845-336-8447
www.casanctuary.org

Eastern Shore Sanctuary and Education Center
158 Massey Road
Springfield, VT 05156
802-885-4017
www.bravebirds.org

Farm Sanctuary, Watkins Glen
P.O. Box 150
Watkins Glen, NY 14891
607-583-2225
www.farmsanctuary.org

Farm Sanctuary, Orland
19080 Newville Road
Orland, CA 95963
530-865-4617
www.farmsanctuary.org

Kindred Spirits Sanctuary
339 SE 54th Court
Ocala, FL 34471
352-629-0009
www.kindredspiritssanctuary.org

Lighthouse Farm Sanctuary
7500 Wallace Road
Salem, OR 97304
503-581-0122
www.lighthousefarmsanctuary.org

Peaceful Prairie Sanctuary
81503 E. County Road 22
Deer Trail, CO 80105
303-769-4997
www.peacefulprairie.org

Poplar Spring Animal Sanctuary
15200 M. Nebo Road
Poolsville, MD 20837
301-428-8128
www.animalsanctuary.org

SASHA Farm
17901 Mahrle
Manchester, MI 48158
734-428-9617
www.sashafarm.org

Serenity Springs Sanctuary
2162 Merritt Road
Forestburg, TX 76239
940-964-2319
www.serenityspringssanctuary.org

Woodstock Farm Animal Sanctuary
P.O. Box 1329
Woodstock, NY 12498
845-679-5955
www.woodstockfas.org

Resources

Organizations

Animal Legal Defense Fund
www.aldf.org

Animal Rights International
www.ari-online.org

Animal Welfare Advocacy
www.animalwelfareandadvocacy.org

Animal Welfare Institute
www.awionline.org

Association of Veterinarians for
Animal Rights
www.avar.org

Compassionate Consumers
www.compassionateconsumers.org

Compassion in World Farming
www.ciwf.org
www.animalsentience.com

Ethologists for the Ethical Treatment
of Animals
www.ethologicalethics.org

Fund for Animals
www.fundforanimals.org

Global Action Network
www.gan.ca

Humane Society of the United States
www.hsus.org

Humane Society Youth
www.humanesocietyyouth.org

Humane USA
www.humaneusa.org

In Defense of Animals
www.idausa.org

"Our task must be to free ourselves . . . by widening our circle of compassion to embrace all living creatures."

—Albert Einstein

164

International Council of Ethologists
www.zoology.ufl.edu/ice/

International Fund for Animal Welfare
www.ifaw.org

International Society for
Applied Ethology
www.applied-ethology.org

Jane Goodall Institute
www.janegoodall.org

Mercy for Animals
www.mercyforanimals.org

National Institute for Animal Advocacy
www.nifaa.org

People for the Ethical Treatment
of Animals
www.peta.org

Physicians Committee for
Responsible Medicine
www.pcrm.org

Roots and Shoots
www.rootsandshoots.org

Royal Society for the Prevention
of Cruelty to Animals
www.rspca.org

Sentient Beings: A Farm Sanctuary
Campaign
www.sentientbeings.org

United Poultry Concerns
www.upc-online.org

World Society for the
Protection of Animals
www.wspa-usa.org
www.wspafarmwelfare.org

"We want to move toward a relationship with farm animals that is not based on violence and domination, but rather that is based on compassion and respect. These animals are social individuals who care about what happens to them, whose mental lives we have dramatically underestimated, and most importantly, who are capable of suffering."

—Paul Shapiro, senior director, Factory Farming Campaign,
The Humane Society of the United States

Books

Balcolmbe, Jonathan. *Pleasurable Kingdom: Animals and the Nature of Feeling Good*. New York, NY: Macmillan, 2006.

Baur, Gene. *Farm Sanctuary: Changing Hearts and Minds About Animals and Food*. New York, NY: Touchstone, 2008.

Bekoff, Marc. *Animals Matter: A Biologist Explains Why We Should Treat Animals with Compassion and Respect*. Boston, MA: Shembhala Publication, 2007.

Bekoff, Marc. *The Emotional Lives of Animals: A Leading Scientist Explores Animal Joy, Sorrow, and Empathy—and Why They Matter*. Novato, CA: New World Library, 2007.

Bekoff, Marc. *Strolling with Our Kin: Speaking for and Respecting Voiceless Animals*. Jenkintown, PA: American Anti-Vivisection Society, 2000.

Davis, Karen. *More Than a Meal: The Turkey in History, Myth, Ritual, and Reality*. New York, NY: Lantern Books, 2001.

Dawn, Karen. *Thanking the Monkey: Rethinking the Way We Treat Animals*. New York, NY: Harper Collins, 2008.

Goodall, Jane. *Harvest for Hope: A Guide to Mindful Eating*. New York, NY: Warner Books, 2005.

Goodall, Jane and Marc Bekoff. *The Ten Trusts: What We Must Do to Care for the Animals We Love*. New York, NY: HarperOne, 2003.

Grandin, Temple and Catherine Johnson. *Animals in Translation: Using the Mysteries of Autism to Decode Animal Behavior*. New York, NY: Scribner, 2005.

Hutto, Joe. *Illumination in the Flatwoods: A Season with the Wild Turkey*. Guilford, CT: The Lyons Press, 2006.

Masson, Jeffrey Moussaieff. *The Pig Who Sang to the Moon*. New York, NY: Random House, Inc., 2003.

Regan, Tom. *The Case for Animal Rights*. Berkeley, CA: University of California Press, 2004.

Regan, Tom. *Empty Cages: Facing the Challenge of Animal Rights*. Lanham, MD: Rowman and Littlefield, 2004.

Scully, Matthew. *Dominion: The Power of Man, the Suffering of Animals, and the Call to Mercy*. New York, NY: St. Martin's Press, 2003.

Singer, Peter. *Animal Liberation*. New York, NY: Harper Perennial, 2001.

Singer, Peter. *In Defense of Animals: The Second Wave*. New York, NY: Wiley-Blackwell, 2005.

Smith, Page and Charles Daniel. *The Chicken Book*. Athens, GA: University of Georgia Press, 2000.

Stallwood, Kim W. *Speaking Out for Animals: True Stories About Real People Who Rescue Animals*. New York, NY: Lantern Books, 2001.

Stevens, Kathy. *Where the Blind Horse Sings: Love and Healing at an Animal Sanctuary*. New York, NY: Skyhorse Publishing, 2007.

Webster, John. *Animal Welfare: Limping Towards Eden*. New York, NY: Wiley-Blackwell, 2005.

Young, Rosamund. *The Secret Life of Cows*. Preston, Lancashire, U.K.: Farming Books & Videos Ltd., 2003.

For Children and Educators

Cultivating Compassion: Teachers' Guide and Student Activities
Lesson plans, handouts, and activities about the sentience of farm animals for third to twelfth grades. Free to teachers at www.farmsanctuary.org.

The Emotional World of Farm Animals
A curriculum and study guide that accompanies the film, *The Emotional World of Farm Animals*. Free to teachers at www.animalplace.org.

Social Change Resource
Campaign materials for schools as well as individuals and groups to help bring about social change for farm animals. Teacher guides and up to twenty copies of the student booklet are available free to schools at www.ciwf.org.

VIDEOS FOR CHILDREN

Farm Animals and Us
This video about farm animal welfare for young children, and *Farm Animals & Us 2,* for ages fourteen and older, are both available at www.ciwf.org.

Let's Ask the Animals
Produced by the Association for the Study of Animal Behavior in conjunction with scientists from Cambridge and Bristol Universities, this video about the intellectual, social, and emotional capacities of farm animals is free for schools at www.ciwf.org.

My Friends on the Farm
Narrated by Casey Affleck, this video for children in third to eighth grades provides an introduction to the realities of factory farming. Available at www.farmsanctuary.org.

Association for the Study of Animal Behavior: Stimulus Response
A video portraying the capacities of farm animals. Available at www.ciwf.org.

BOOKS FOR CHILDREN AND YOUTH

A Home for Henny
Written by Karen Davis and illustrated by Patricia Vandenbergh, this is the story of a child who rescues a chicken from a school project. Available at www.upc-online.org.

Going Vegan: A Veggie Starter Kit for Teens
This comic book written by dietitian Jack Norris is available online or can be ordered for free from www.animalplace.org.

Justice for All
This comic is about a pig living on a factory farm who leads the other animals on a revolt. Available at www.animalplace.org.

Smarter Than Jack
Created by Jenny Campbell, this series of true animal stories from around the world is available at www.smarterthanjack.com.

Where Magical Things Happen
Written by Kim Sterla and illustrated by Eric Sakach, this book introduces children aged five through eight to the concepts of compassion and respect for animals. Available at www.animalplace.org.

"**Children see all the similarities between humans and animals.**"

—Bernard E. Rollins

Bibliography

Bekoff, Marc, Colin Allen, and Gordon Burghardt, eds. *The Cognitive Animal: Empirical and Theoretical Perspectives on Animal Cognition*. Cambridge, MA: The MIT Press, 2002.

Bekoff, Marc and Dale Jamieson, eds. *Readings in Animal Cognition*. Cambridge, MA: The MIT Press, 2006.

Broom, Donald M. *The Evolution of Morality and Religion*. Cambridge, U.K.: The University Press, 2003.

Broom, Donald M., and A. F. Fraser. *Domestic Animal Behavior and Welfare* (Fourth Edition). London, U.K.: CABI, 2007.

Broom, Donald Maurice. "The Evolution of Morality." *Applied Animal Behavior Science* 100 (2006): 20–28.

Darwin, Charles, *The Expression of the Emotions in Man and Animals*. Oxford, U.K.: Oxford University Press, 1998.

Davis, Karen. *Prisoned Chickens, Poisoned Eggs: An inside look at the modern poultry industry*. Summertown, TN: Book Publishing Company, 1996.

Dawkins, Marian Stamp. *Through Our Eyes Only?: The Search for Animal Consciousness*. Oxford, U.K.: Oxford University Press, 1998.

"Ducks quack in regional accents." BBC News Online, June 4, 2004. http://news.bbc.co.uk/cbbcnews/hi/animal/newsid_3776000/3776023.stm.

Farm Sanctuary, "Sentient Beings: A Summary of the Scientific Evidence Establishing Sentience in Farmed Animals."

Fraser, A. F. *Farm Animal Behavior and Welfare* (Third Edition). London, U.K.: CABI, 1996.

Griffin, Donald. *Animal Minds: Beyond Cognition to Consciousness*. Chicago, IL: University of Chicago Press, 1992.

Hagen, Kristin and Donald M. Broom. "Emotional Reactions to Learning in Cattle." *Applied Animal Behavior Science* 85 (2004): 203–213.

Held, S., J. J. Cooper, and M. Mendl. "Advances in the study of cognition, behavioural needs and emotions." *The Welfare of Pigs*. Ed. J. Marchant Forde. Norwell, MA: Kluwer Academic Publishers.

Held, S. and M. Mendl. 2001. "Behaviour of the young weaner pig." *The Weaner Pig*. Eds. Wiseman, J. and M. Varley. Oxfordshire, U.K.: CABI.

Hrdy, Sarah Blaffer. *Mother Nature. Maternal Instincts and How They Shape the Human Species*. New York, NY: Ballantine Books, 2000.

Jensen, P. *The Ethology of Domestic Animals: An Introductory Text* (First Edition). London, U.K.: CABI, 2002.

Keeling, L. J., and H. W. Gonyou, eds. *Social Behavior in Farm Animals*. London, U.K.: CABI, 2001.

Kendrick, Keith M. "Intelligent Perception." *Applied Animal Behavior Science* 57 (1998): 213–231.

Nicol, Christine. "How Animals Learn from Each Other." *Applied Animal Behavior Science* 100 (2006): 58–63.

Rifkin, Jeremy. "Man and Other Animals." *Guardian Unlimited* (August, 2003).

Rogers, Lesley J. *Minds of their Own: Thinking and Awareness in Animals*. Boulder, CO: Westview Press, 1998.

Rogers, Lesley J. *The Development of Brain and Behavior in the Chicken*. Oxfordshire, U.K.: CABI, 1996.

Turner, Jackie and Joyce D'Silva, eds. *Animals, Ethics and Trade: The Challenge of Animal Sentience*. London, U.K.: Earthscan, 2006.

Turner, Jacky. "Stop, Look, Listen: Recognising the Sentience of Farm Animals." Compassion in World Farming Trust, 2006.

Wemelsfelder, Francoise, et al. "Assessing the 'Whole Animal': A Free Choice Profiling Approach." *Animal Behaviour* 62 (2001): 209–220.

Acknowledgments

Writing *The Inner World of Farm Animals* has been a profound experience, not only because of what I have learned and how it has changed me, but also because of the people I have met along the way. The book has been blessed with an extraordinary village to help raise it.

I want to express my profound gratitude to Dr. Jane Goodall for gracing this book with her clear and compassionate voice that has forever changed the world for animals. My appreciation also to Christin Jones and Mary Lewis of the Jane Goodall Institute for their patience and help. I'd like to express my heartfelt appreciation to Wayne Pacelle, one of the country's strongest advocates for animals, who took time out of his valiant fight for Prop 2 in California to write the afterword for this book. My thanks also to Bernie Unti for his wise suggestions and edits.

I am grateful to Joyce D'Silva, ambassador for Compassion in World Farming (CIWF), for all that she does and for all that she gave to this book. Heartfelt thanks also to Wendy Smith at CIWF, who never said no.

My thanks to the founders and staff members of farm animal sanctuaries across the country. Gene Baur, president and co-founder of Farm Sanctuary, was my first introduction to the amazingly dedicated, devoted, and compassionate nature of people rescuing and saving the lives of farm animals. They are like angels on earth, and they gave their time, their wisdom, their stories, and their photographs to the book. They include Doug Abel, Jenny Brown, Susie Coston, Terry Cummings, Pattrice Jones, Norm Scott, Kim Sterla, and Kathy Stevens. A special thanks to Karen Davis, founder and president of United Poultry Concerns and to Rosamund Young from Kites Nest Farm.

I am grateful to Bob Esposito who generously donated his exquisite photographs, which capture the souls and personalities of the animals and melt the hearts of everyone who sees them.

My profound appreciation to all of the scientists and researchers whose work informs the bulk of this book. And a special thanks to those who spent time walking me through their research and offering feedback on the manuscript. They include Jack Albright, Derek Bailey, Candace Croney, Sam Gosling, William Healy, Suzanne Held, Joe Hutto, Keith Kendrick, Mike Mendl, Ed Pajor, Lesley Rogers, Joe Stookey, and Giorgio Vallaritigaro.

Many thanks to my friends and family members who watched over me, cheered me on, or just listened. They include Susan and Alan Patricof, Marcia Patricof, Lisa Selsby Cohler,

Susan Jacobsen, John Schnall, Susan Wolf, Satya Kirsch, Gay French-Ottaviani, Arlene Hellerman, and Les Borden. A special thanks to Kemal Dural who shared the magic of the animals and captured it in hundreds of photographs.

My gratitude to a fantastic support team who joined me in this journey and helped me reach the finish line. They include Kimberly Bastion, Cat Clyne, James Kuslan, Jennifer Souisian, Dawn Perry, Minda Novek, and Dana Devine O'Malley. Thanks also to Martin Rowe of Lantern Books for his keen ear and sharp edits.

A very special thanks to my agent, Carolyn French, a true animal lover, who keeps me on track with her words of wisdom and continues to recognize and nurture the writer in me.

Thanks to my publisher, Stewart, Tabori & Chang, for again bringing my work to life and to Anna Christian, who materialized my vision with her exquisite design. And finally, my heartfelt thanks to my editor, Kristen Latta, who carries within her a deep affinity, love, and concern for all animals. When she first read the pencil-marked, wrinkled draft of the proposal, she cried. From that moment she has remained committed, shepherding the book along and carrying the torch that it hopes to light.

Photo Credits

"Any glimpse into the life of an animal quickens our own and makes it so much the larger and better in every way."

—John Muir